NEGOTI
SIX STEPS
TO SUCCESS

Michael A. Walker
and
George L. Harris

For book and bookstore information

http://www.prenhall.com

PTR Prentice Hall
Upper Saddle River, NJ 07458

Library of Congress Cataloging-in-Publication Data

Walker, Michael A.
Negotiations: six steps to success / Michael A. Walker, George L. Harris.
   p. cm.
   Includes bibliographical references and index.
   ISBN 0-13-125592-4
   1. Negotiation in business. 2. Negotiation. I. Harris, George L. II. Title.
HD58.6.W34 1995   95–18030
658.4--dc20   CIP

Acquisitions Editor: Bernard Goodwin
Cover design: Anthony Gemmellaro
Cover photo: 1994, Comstock
Manufacturing manager: *Alexis Heydt*
Editorial/production supervision: *Benchmark Productions*

© 1995 by Prentice Hall PTR
Prentice-Hall Inc.
A Pearson Education Company
Upper Saddle River, NJ 07458

The publisher offers discounts on this book when ordered
in bulk quantities. For more information contact:

Corporate Sales Department
Prentice Hall PTR
One Lake Street
Upper Saddle River, NJ 07458
Phone: 800-382-3419 Fax: 201-236-7141
E-mail: corpsales@prenhall.com

Printed in the United States of America
10   9   8   7   6   5   4   3   2   1

ISBN 0-13-125592-4

Prentice-Hall International (UK) Limited,London
Prentice-Hall of Australia Pty. Limited, Sydney
Prentice-Hall Canada Inc., Toronto
Prentice-Hall Hispanoamericana, S.A., Mexico
Prentice-Hall of India Private Limited, New Delhi
Prentice-Hall of Japan, Inc., Tokyo
Pearson Education Asia Pte. Ltd., Singapore
Editora Prentice-Hall do Brasil, Ltda., Rio de Janeiro

To our families, who have taught us to negotiate in good faith with a vision toward win-win conclusions

Contents

C H A P T E R   3 **Getting Ready:**
                  Analyzing the Negotiation Situation   41

C H A P T E R   7   **Getting it Done: Closing Negotiations   111**

Preface

This book offers a simple, systematic approach to a subject that can be complex, daunting, and full of surprises—the art and technique of negotiation. While we are often aware of and impressed by the celebrated negotiators of the world; government representatives, athletes, or entertainers; all of us are called upon at some point to pick up the gauntlet and attempt to settle a difference by amiable discussion.

Our ability to negotiate competently affects every aspect of our life and work; the prices we pay for capital purchases and real estate, the procurement of loans, career moves, and the happiness of the people around us. So why have we overlooked developing this skill and why do we have such difficulty negotiating? We, the authors, believe that individuals lack a dependable and effective process to accomplish negotiations. We wrote this book to provide such a process to anyone who wishes to negotiate anything.

We recognized a need for simplifying what seems to many to be a complex and often intimidating process. We thus separated the negotiating process into six manageable phases which, if followed carefully, will lead to successful resolution of dispute. The model we have developed can be used as a skeleton for analyzing and planning the simplest negotiation or as a structure on which to build a plan for the most complex, team-bargaining session.

Our model covers the spectrum of activity from preliminary planning to negotiation discussion to post-agreement and continuous improvement efforts. We believe that our six step approach provides the individual with the opportunity to refine his or her negotiating skills, regardless of negotiation history.

One advantage of our model is that it divides pre-negotiation planning into three distinct steps. The first step concentrates on the strategic goals of the negotiation. The near-term or tactical objective is determined in the second step. In the third step, detailed plans and agendas are developed. The remaining three steps lead one through the actual negotiation phase. They concern gaining and maintaining control, closing negotiations, and continuous improvement techniques for reviewing performance. The most important benefit of this six step approach is that it provides the negotiator with a clear and definite outline for action that keeps the major, strategic goals in the forefront of the negotiation process.

This book, then, is about negotiation, a process that is universally practiced, but seldom mastered. We would like negotiators to be satisfied with their results. This is not to suggest that all negotiations should have a win/win outcome—sometimes there must be a loser. But we believe the techniques and attitudes required for win/win negotiation—clear communications, empathy, awareness of the opposition's interests, and a sense of fair play—will help the opposition to see the advantage of compromise, even if one's original objectives are not achieved.

With our 25 years of experience in training thousands of negotiators in the U.S. and abroad, we trust that readers will gain from this book and improve their future negotiations. We've exerted great effort to make this book easy to read and apply and with the concrete techniques, templates, case studies, and real-life examples that we have used, we hope the negotiation process comes to life for you. We wish all of you the best of negotiating in your future endeavors.

Lexington, Massachusetts
February, 1995

About the Authors

George Harris, president and founder of Harris Consulting, is deeply involved in training and consulting over a broad spectrum of functional expertise. In addition to holding senior management positions at Digital Equipment, Prime Computer and Arthur D. Little, he was part of the Harbridge House consulting team for a number of years. His clients have ranged from major firms such as General Electric, Hughes, Pratt & Whitney and Raytheon to start-up firms and small businesses.

Mr Harris has specialized in management training in the areas of contract management, purchasing and negotiations. He has taught hundreds of negotiators in the U.S. and abroad and has developed a specialized practice in the areas of continuous improvement, TQM and ISO-9000 registrations.

A graduate of Georgetown and George Washington Universities, he resides in Lexington, Massachusetts.

Mike Walker is a writer and management consultant who has specialized in technical communications and related fields for over 30 years. The creator of many innovative training vehicles such as cases, workshops, role plays, simulations and analytical exercises, he has trained literally thousands of executives, managers, and practicing negotiators. As a key player at Boston-based Harbridge House for many years his major clients have included General Electric, IBM, MacDonald's, Raytheon, Rockwell, Sprint, UTC, Westinghouse, Xerox and many Federal agencies. He has developed a special proficiency in cost analysis and is nationally known for his expertise with contract incentives.

A graduate of Harvard University with an MBA from Suffolk University, Mr. Walker resides in Sudbury and Sandwich, Massachusetts. He is presently associated with Harris Consulting of Lexington, MA.

Acknowledgments

To the late Harvey White, Vice President of United Technologies, who inspired us to train his organization on the value of intrinsic worth in negotiations.

To Arnold Lovering, Manager of Purchasing Programs at Raytheon Company, who provided constructive feedback on our six-step model and the need for hands-on examples.

To those business professionals who completed our Negotiation Questionnaires, which provided an overview of various approaches and specific case studies on results achieved.

To our current and previous customers, who challenged us to provide value-added training programs to their employees with a view in applying acquired skills on the job.

To the writers of previously written material on negotiations and conflict management, all of which provided a baseline for our thinking on the subject and who drive us to further excellence in the area.

Toward a Process View of Negotiations

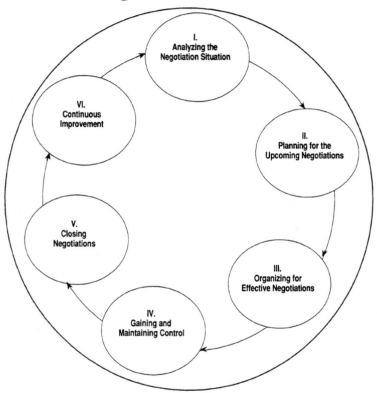

1.1 PUT YOURSELF IN THIS POSITION

You are selling your primary residence after 30 years and moving to Cape Cod with your husband. You have invested a substantial amount of personal and financial capital in your home over the years, and have raised four children in it. Although you want to sell the house to the "right" buyer who could experience the same excitement, thrills, and family culture as you have, the price has to be significant enough to pay for your condo on Cape Cod. What do you do now? Your response to this question depends on how experienced you are in planning for negotiations, how comfortable you are in confronting others, and how persuasive you can be in getting your points across to others.

This book is about negotiation—a process that is universally practiced but seldom mastered. Our purpose is to make our readers better negotiators by raising their comfort level with the subject. Using our years of experience in training many types of managers in negotiations and conflict resolution, we will try to remove some of the mystique that surrounds this intriguing activity. We will also challenge the current paradigms about negotiations and offer some new ones more suited to the current environment. We have devised a simple, systematic approach to planning and executing successful negotiations. We will illustrate the importance of a disciplined approach to accomplishing negotiations and will provide some proven techniques for achieving such discipline.

Our method is simple and practical, with less emphasis on theory than we have observed in other treatments of this subject. Our goal is to provide a structure that negotiators, both new and experienced, can use with confidence while developing approaches to otherwise daunting negotiation challenges.

1.2 SOME COMMON PERCEPTIONS

In the broadest sense negotiation may be defined as the process of resolving differences through mutually acceptable tradeoffs. To most, this connotes compromise but to many it presumes that someone has won an advantage and that there is a loser as well as a winner. This could be due to our competitive nature or how we have been trained. It is fair to say, however, that most people assume that they are not very good negotiators and are somewhat envious of those who are. Human beings are basically afraid of *losing*. We should all view negotiations as an opportunity to gain, not to lose.

Have you ever had the experience, in a friendly game of stud poker, of folding in the face of an apparent straight or flush only to find that the other party was bluffing? Or have you a friend who always tends to get better deals on cars, houses, and antiques than you do? Or have you seen the person who can show up on a busy night at the most exclusive restaurant in town and immediately be seated at a table with a perfect view, while you must wait for a spot near the kitchen? Of course, in the latter case, a bit of bribery may have been involved. But the perception is that the people who pull off such coups are the champion negotiators of the world and we'd hate to meet them across a bargaining table. We are also painfully aware that it is a display of bravado and sheer self-confidence that often carries the day. This success, however, is often due to the quality of the negotiator's planning and execution of a pre-ordained strategy. But we all would like to have that kind of charisma, or gall, or whatever it is!

The value of such personal traits in attaining negotiation success is a given. It is a basic premise of this book, however, that one can be an effective negotiator without being the smoothest character since Errol Flynn. The key is a simple system for developing a plan for negotiating particular issues and a method for carrying it out. We will point out vivid examples of this system throughout this book.

The posturing and positioning that achieves success in certain interpersonal situations is a subtle form of negotiating that would require deep personality analysis to be understood. On the other hand, the more structured type of interchange that often occurs in settling a real difference can be analyzed in a more precise, straightforward way. Many people appear to relish such confrontations while others don't find them to be much fun. Most of us cringe at the thought of the weird mating dance that seems obligatory at car buying time. Few situations are more traumatic than closing a deal on a home (either selling or buying) for the fear of getting "taken" in a high stakes game with enormous long-term financial impact.

While there are many who abhor such situations, there are others (surely a minority) who revel in the excitement of the give-and-take and coming out on top. To give and take effectively requires up-front planning and the discipline of following through and sticking to the plan during negotiations. Besting an opponent through the expert application of proven negotiation techniques can be a peak experience. When such successes occur in business situations, careers can be made or broken. Smaller, though no less enjoyable victories, can be won in less formal circumstances such as yard sales or antique shopping, and even securing more favorable terms from one's landlord. In all situations good negotiation practice can be useful and even fun. It is the more formal business situations, however, which most severely test our negotiation skills and these will be the primary focus of this book.

1.3 NEED FOR A STRUCTURED APPROACH

Although opportunities for applying one's bargaining technique can arise almost anywhere in our daily routine, it is on the job where our negotiation abilities are most severely challenged. Whether it be interviewing for a job, reaching agreement on salary or employment terms, allocating internal resources effectively, obtaining a fair price from a vendor, working out a long-term agreement with a major supplier, or ensuring excellent service from the company that leases your copying machines—all of these situations demand the same sensitivity and self-assurance that our day-to-day interactions with others require. But for some reason we tend to feel less confident in these structured business confrontations.

Why do many of us tense up and avoid such activities unless our job requirements leave us no choice but to deal with them? One possible reason is our lack of a systematic method for confronting the expertise that we presume our business associate (adversary?) to possess. In the absence of a routinized methodical approach to negotiations we are forced to follow a hit-or-miss, seat-of-the-pants strategy in which we react to challenges presented, rather than proactively creating opportunities for ourselves. As a result, we are often less confident that we have reached the best or optimal results at the conclusion of a negotiation.

We believe that effective negotiation can be achieved by using a simple system for planning and executing negotiations. Such a system will be useful in all negotiating situations—whether a single-issue verbal exchange over the phone or a multifaceted confrontation involving several participants, numerous issues, and face-to-face meetings in a relatively formal setting. Our approach is to utilize the classic principles of planning and execution employed by managers of complex projects and programs throughout industry. By concentrating on the critical elements of the planning model we have created a simple step-by-step procedure to be followed intuitively in the simplest of negotiations as well as the large-scale, high-stakes affairs. The confidence that will be generated by following the simple steps will encourage boldness and self-assurance in presenting one's position in the best possible light. We will utilize a template of key activities to be accomplished in each step so that users can keep track.

Our principles apply to the negotiation process just as those classic management functions that are taught to managers from day one—planning, organizing, staffing, and controlling. This is hardly a revolutionary idea, but our perception is that most writers and teachers in the negotiation field ignore these basic principles in favor of the dramatics, psychological factors, and tactical nuances of the negotiation exchange. We agree that these subtleties are important, and certainly entertaining, but can be more profitably understood and employed in the context of a structured negotiation plan. In our view, such a plan must be created in discrete logical steps that reflect sound management practice. At the same time, the plan must lend itself to continuous improvement practices in accordance with the Deming philosophy prevalent today.

1.4 ADOPTING A NEW PARADIGM

Good negotiators are born not made. Those individuals who can negotiate well possess the personality traits and temperament to secure the best results for their cause. Just look at how Lee Iocacca was able to extract billions from the federal government to save

Chrysler. Consider the skills of Peter Uberroth when he negotiated the record setting business arrangements for the Summer Olympics in Los Angeles. If you are impressed with these examples and accept the assertion made at the outset of this paragraph, you have unfortunately fallen victim to the power of the most prevalent *paradigm* about negotiations.

Paradigms are patterns and rules that people use to justify and rationalize their behavior. Examples of well known paradigms are:

- People don't want to hear voices in movies.
- Women will never vote.
- Desktop computing is a fad.

From these examples we can see that many paradigms are short-lived, while others prove useful and stand up over time. Then there are cynical paradigms expressed in terms of "that will never work" or "we've always done it this way." This is especially true in negotiations since most of the learning and training concerning negotiations is done on a personal basis between current and potential negotiators.

Paradigms are used by people because they provide the rationale or a logic system for following a specific course of action. They frequently encourage inherently less risky alternatives because the majority of individuals accept the currently popular paradigm or they are either unwilling or incapable of challenging the existing school of thought. But paradigms are dangerous: they impose an arbitrary standard or thought pattern on our activities to the point of thwarting creativity, innovation, and probably more importantly, *progress*.

Paradigms abound in negotiations because relationships and, to a certain extent, ultimate success are private or personal matters. This is fostered by word of mouth success factors, organizational responsibilities for the negotiation effort itself, and the desire of individuals to have guidelines on activities which are less tangible than those that can be proceduralized.

1.5 EXAMPLES OF PARADIGMS IN NEGOTIATIONS

In years of training thousands of managers and individual contributors in the skills of effective negotiation, we have observed that, by far, the most prevalent paradigm is that the skills to become an effective negotiator cannot be learned. People believe that good negotiators are blessed with the preexisting skills and personality traits to be effective. Although some people do exhibit a tendency to enjoy bartering and negotiating more than others, they do so because they have developed a process or methodology which works for them and guides them through the negotiations. As they gain more experience, this methodology becomes more intuitive as they begin to follow mental rather than written prompts to accomplish their negotiation objectives.

In many of our training programs, participants tell us, or the groups in which they work, that they are experienced negotiators, that they have been to the "school of hard knocks," or that they have their own personalized approach which is successful. It is these same individuals who have the most difficulty in the negotiating exercises. Why? One could postulate that it is due to a built-in bias against classroom training or maybe the fictitious nature of a simulated role-play. We believe that people don't realize that negotiation requires a rigorous accomplishment of tasks. This is why they are "stumped" about what to do next. We believe that these tasks can be learned and practiced.

Although "Negotiation" is offered in some MBA or law degree curricula, it generally is not given the emphasis it deserves in business or law school programs. Most people are not exposed to it, and as with conflict management, people are expected to just "do it," manage it, take care of it. This lack of focus or the availability of a forum or environment to gain the required process knowledge creates a specific need to learn the skills and principles of negotiations.

There also are individuals who exude quite a bit of confidence in their negotiating ability. This confidence perhaps makes up for some of the deficiencies created by the lack of a defined approach. More often than not these individuals are not as successful as they might have been, had they used a specific template or methodology.

Based upon our experience, we find that individuals can learn specific methodologies to help them accomplish successful negotiations. After following those methodologies a number of times and learning through experiences, individuals can become very practiced negotiators. The paradigm that you can't learn to be an effective negotiator should not be so readily accepted.

Another response that we frequently hear when asking people to negotiate more is that negotiation means confrontation. We have found that a significant number of individuals do not like confronting others: they view confrontation as a potentially negative experience since reputations and personal egos are at stake.

When the United States "negotiated" with Fidel Castro and Cuba during the missile crisis in the early 1960s, terms were confused as we "negotiated" with Castro and Kruschev, then "confronted" them with the issues. The ultimate sign of confrontation, indelible in the minds of many, was the sight of American armed naval vessels blocking Cuba-bound ships which might have had armaments on them.

We confused the notion of negotiations—where parties attempt to exchange items of value in an effort to reach agreement on a final outcome—with the concept of confrontation—where one party points out information or behavior to another in an effort to escalate the controversy to reach resolution. In the so-called Cuban crisis, we did *confront* the Cubans and Soviets on the existence of missile sites in Cuba. We did try to negotiate their dismantlement. When it failed, we confronted them with the establishment of a blockade which was an act of escalation to force the other party to react in kind. Although confrontation is often found in negotiations, particularly involving negotiators who have an antagonistic or negative style, it is through the application of appropriate tactics that the tenor of the negotiations can be changed from confrontation to cooperation.

It is also important to recognize that confrontation is a regularly practiced negotiating style and can be used effectively against you if you do not counter it in some way. Having a legitimate process to employ allows the negotiator to use an independent, objective standard to move the negotiations from confrontation to a more acceptable plane.

In many companies, only senior managers negotiate the important business arrangements and deals. Often, there are dollar limitations governing who eventually negotiates. These practices and procedures foster an acceptance of the idea that only managers and high ranking individuals negotiate, thus denying to many contributors opportunities to control their own destinies. One can understand why there are dollar limitations but there are no built-in assurances, or data for that matter, that managers are more effective negotiators than individual contributors. Yet this paradigm endures in corporations. The existence of this practice reduces the confidence of individuals who are thrust into negotiation situations normally carried out by managers, produces unsatisfactory results, and increases individuals' uncertainty regarding their own personal capability.

In actuality, we believe that non-managers often negotiate more frequently or more effectively than managers. Because a worker often has an immediate task to finish, he/she must learn to negotiate quickly to reconcile problems and remove obstacles. It is only when these individuals cannot negotiate to a successful conclusion that the manager is asked to negotiate with his/her counterpart. We have seen little evidence to suggest that managers are better at negotiations or that they achieve better results. What we have observed is that successful managers are extremely effective communicators. This skill allows them to present information and data to others in a persuasive and knowledgeable way. This fact alone does not make them better negotiators, as they still follow a prescribed process to reach successful results. What should be ensured is the acceptance of a bona fide negotiation process which all negotiators follow and learn from so that anyone thrust into negotiations can have the same level of confidence that successful results can be achieved.

There are significant differences among individuals in the amount of aggressiveness they exhibit in negotiations. This is due to natural tendencies in individuals, their degree of competitiveness, and the personal commitment and investment they have made to accomplish the objectives sought by the negotiations. Aggressiveness, if properly applied, should enhance an individual's commitment and desire to accomplish a negotiation result whereby both parties win. Unfortunately, many negotiators are strongly driven to win, thus having a sharp focus on a short-term win while jeopardizing their position in the long term.

One of our clients sought our assistance in softening the approach of their purchasing personnel whose aggressive negotiating style was hurting the company's image among suppliers and vendors.

More seriously, in some cases contracts were being negotiated downward in price to the extent that suppliers could not live up to their agreements, thus endangering established manufacturing schedules of the buying firm. In one particularly egregious case, our client firm was forced, under difficult time constraints, to locate an alternate source for a crucial item. An inflated price had to be paid since the supplier who had received the original order was unable to meet the difficult specifications he had agreed to. Thus the elation the buyer had felt at his exciting win turned to bitter disappointment when the victory turned sour.

The last paradigm to be covered is that an effective negotiations process is difficult to learn. The words "process" or "methodology" can be viewed as implying a difficult, convoluted, and perhaps confusing set of steps or procedures.

Most of us learn to drive a car. Yet, in the early stages of gaining knowledge and experience we are given a set of instructions either by the State Registry of Motor Vehicles or by our driving "instructor." At first blush, these instructions are both lengthy and specific:

- Sit comfortably in seat
- Turn the ignition
- Look both ways
- Put the car in gear
- Turn the wheel
- Apply the brake
- Look at the rear view mirror
- etc., etc.

Once we have gained experience, we naturally follow these steps and they become ingrained in our daily routine. We believe that the steps we are offering, once practiced, can be followed intuitively. Our method is a series of easy-to-follow, logical steps that will allow you to achieve positive results. The process is not an end in itself, but rather a tool to use and change as necessary to help plan and manage the negotiations.

1.6 WHY THESE PARADIGMS MUST CHANGE

People need to feel empowered to negotiate. The paradigms discussed in this chapter produce the opposite result. To wit:

- Personal confidence in one's ability to negotiate is lacking.
- The responsibility to negotiate is frequently passed on to another party.
- The negotiations process is considered confusing and difficult to learn.
- The ability of individuals to accomplish their goals is compromised.

It must be recognized that everyone negotiates in some shape or form, at one time or another; the results of our negotiations vary remarkably from person to person. Since we all do negotiate, we must search for a paradigm which will increase our potential for becoming effective negotiators. We believe that our method counters most of these negotiation paradigms and puts negotiation success within the reach of anyone willing to try. We must begin to adopt a view that negotiation skills can be learned by everyone. An excellent start is to learn and apply a standardized approach to accomplish the negotiations.

1.7 WHY THIS BOOK?

To the reader whose reaction to this effort is "Not another book on negotiation!" we request your indulgence and offer the following. We believe our structured step-by-step approach to planning and conducting negotiations is unique and particularly useful to inexperienced negotiators. On the other hand, the procedure will aid the most experienced negotiator by providing a framework for laying out a position and a plan for attaining it.

Another distinguishing feature of this book is its focus on realistic standards of negotiation success. We are well aware of the significant contributions of writers such as Karass, Nierenburg, Fisher and Ury, Freund, and many others. Indeed, Chester Karass "wrote the book" and with many others enriched the professionals' understanding of the art of negotiation, particularly the use of stratagems and tactics. However, among the negotiations community an unhealthy preoccupation with "winning the game" still exists. While there are many factors that contribute to this attitude not a great deal has been written, with the exception of Fisher and Ury's work, about the value of "win/win" negotiations in which both parties walk away achieving some or most of their objectives. What is generally missing from normal approaches is the presentation of a workable template on "how to" accomplish effective negotiation results.

Many business managers deplore the long-term effects of win/lose practices, since the loser very often returns to gain the advantage somewhere down the line. Positive, beneficent relationships with associates are usually in the interests of both parties in search of settlements responding to mutually important needs. It is our intent in this book to inculcate in practitioners a respectful attitude for the other party's interests while presenting their own case in the most effective light. We believe a thorough understanding of the negotiation process and the consistent application of sound execution techniques will make truly professional performance an attainable standard for all negotiators who are willing to try.

In delineating the step-by-step planning procedure that we advocate, we will provide numerous examples to demonstrate the effectiveness of the tactics and actions suggested. These will be drawn from actual cases as well as lessons learned while training thousands of negotiators over the past 25 years.

The Case for a Systematic Negotiating Process

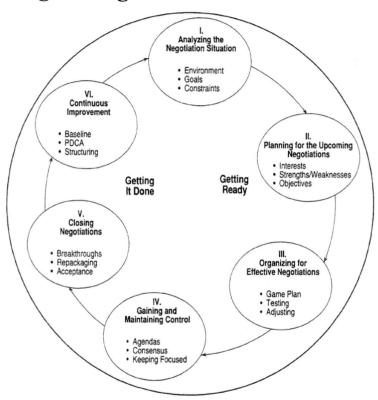

What causes the success of one negotiation and the failure of others? Just what is it that distinguishes good negotiations from bad ones and how can individuals improve the percentages of good results? Much can be learned from previously attempted negotiations; not from an "armchair" quarterback perspective but in performing post–mortem what-if scenarios. True, one could learn from successful negotiations but it is human nature to learn more from failures than from victories.

To find representative examples of negotiations, take a look at any issue of the *Wall Street Journal*. You are apt to find negotiations occurring at all levels; from the announcement of a joint venture to a company attempting a hostile takeover. If you review the paper even more closely, you will find negotiations happening in less obvious ways. Recent examples we have noted include Merrill Lynch's plan to originate large commercial loans and the USX refusal to go along with AK Steel's planned price increase.

Let's look at three examples we gleaned from one recent edition of the *Wall Street Journal*.

2.1 PETRIE STORES SALE TO EMPLOYEES

Petrie Stores was negotiating to sell its retail stores to a group of managers and investors for up to $250 million. In this negotiation, there was clearly a lot at stake for both parties. The ailing owner of the business, Milton Petrie, had recently removed himself from active day-to-day management of the women's clothing store chain and apparently desired to sell to management in an all-equity bid. The managers were hopeful to win the bid because it not only would mean continued employment, but would create the strong balance necessary for future company growth. One can see that since both parties had a strong focused interest in working out an arrangement, a win/win result could be likely. The reporter must have thought so because he quoted one of the potential investors who said, "One of the exciting things about Petrie Stores is that the people who are in top management positions are very hands on, a wonderful group of people." We should be aware of the attitudes of people involved because they can influence the outcome of negotiations, both positively and negatively.

2.2 CONFLICT IN BOSNIA

In a more complex and significant situation, the Bosnian Serbs and Muslim-Croats were approached with a plan to carve up their country according to ethnic lines under a map proposed by negotiators for the U.S., Europe, and Russia. This tri-party negotiation had a number of interesting twists to it:

- Bosnia and Muslim factions could view this as an imposed solution.
- A third party group had devised this solution without consultation.
- Under the proposed plan, the Serbs would have to give up some of the territory that they had won during the war.
- Both sides could feel that they could gain more by continuing to fight.
- The third party negotiators could have had more to lose than the Serbs or Muslim-Croats.
- Third party negotiators in these circumstances often have exhausted many of the tested negotiation strategies and the independently imposed separation of the Bosnian territory might be viewed as a last resort.

For these reasons, chances were very great that the final outcome of the Bosnian conflict would not be solved on the basis of territory agreement but on the reconciliation of differences and a desire to co-exist in Europe. Although both parties believed the worst choice was war, people do what they have to do versus doing what they like to do in wartime situations.

2.3   PRUDENTIAL ENTRY INTO THE MUTUAL FUNDS BUSINESS

The third example in that *Journal* issue was the announcement that Prudential Insurance would begin to sell no-load mutual funds. In our experience, when companies plan new ventures they seldom plan on the resistance to change and new ideas that exist within their own companies. It is accepted management dogma that implementing changes is the most challenging task that companies face. In almost every seminar we teach on negotiations, participants tell us that the toughest, most demanding, and possibly the most frustrating negotiations occur *within* organizations. In our view, this was something Prudential would experience as they began to implement this new strategy.

Internal resistance could be expected because mutual funds are not bought through brokers. This means that the company needed not only to begin to sell these funds directly, which is itself a culture change, but would need to convince the brokers that this made sense from a business perspective while still keeping them interested in the company's other products. Other companies have tried this before. Kemper Corp. finally lost control of the no-load mutual fund group they established when the mutual funds' dissatisfied directors took the assets elsewhere. This upcoming Prudential negotiation thus must be focused on internal parties for resolution, but precedent does not augur well for their success.

2.4   SOME ESSENTIALLY COMPLETED NEGOTIATIONS

From a time perspective, we looked at these three negotiations primarily in the beginning stages. Lets take a look at some essentially completed negotiations and find some lessons learned.

TCI-Bell Atlantic

The first example is that of a failed merger—the proposed TCI-Bell Atlantic "mega-merger" which collapsed in early 1994. These two companies desired to merge to create a communications giant, linking phone lines and cable networks to wire up America along the information superhighway.

The trouble began when the U.S. Federal Trade Commission imposed a 7% cut in the average consumer bill. Amounting to just over $1.45 on a monthly basis, the cut forced the Bell Atlantic Chairman, Raymond W. Smith, to recalculate the offer price for TCI. This reduction was met with unexpected resistance by the TCI Chairman, John C. Malone, and as the parties dug into their positions, the merger was finally scuttled. Bell Atlantic had calculated that for every dollar reduction in the monthly bill, the purchase price for TCI should be reduced by $11.75. This cut the overall purchase price by $1.6 billion and caused the loss of borrowing power of nearly $900 million. Thus, the negotiations ceased due to purely financial terms as opposed to considering the future of the companies and the overall value of their combined capability.

Suppose the parties had taken a more critical view of their goals at the outset and considered the vastly different cultures of the two companies. Bell Atlantic, a staid and highly structured and regulated company, wanted to acquire and negotiate with TCI, which is known as a free-wheeling entrepreneurish cable operator. What did the companies want to gain for themselves and through the joined companies as a result of the merger? This question wasn't addressed by the parties. How do you merge the bi-polar cultures of the companies? This apparently was also not addressed, not only from a result of the merger but as a *component* of the negotiating plan. Ultimately, the negotiations took on the personalities of the companies; Bell-Atlantic was very rigid in its stance and TCI was attempting to try many different, even risky approaches. At one point, it was reported that Mr. Malone told his executives that they "would be out of their minds to accept the current terms" and that he could not "budge a nickel."

This case study provides four important lessons:

1. Be attuned to the cultural and personality differences between the parties and adjust your negotiation plan accordingly, even to the point of replacing the lead negotiator.

2. Try to incorporate non-price or non-financial criteria into your negotiations plan so that you consider all possible benefits to be gained and thus reduce the likelihood of not reaching agreement due to pure financial reasons. (Of course, if the financial issues are of disastrous proportions, they must be controlling.)

3. Never lose focus on your primary objective. Be steadfast in looking long–term. Even though long–term results are harder to measure, they often provide the best ultimate advantage to the negotiating parties. This action requires, however, total awareness of business priorities.

4. Don't polarize yourself or your team by taking a position which offers few, if any, alternatives to agreement. This is particularly applicable if you are the senior member of your group and you are making the statements or leading the negotiations.

U.S.—Japan Trade

Let's look at the status of U.S.—Japan trade negotiation at this writing in 1994. The history of the various attempts at reaching a satisfactory trade agreement with Japan is rich with negotiating ploys, significant "one-liners," political rhetoric and accusations. No matter where you stand in your opinion of the effectiveness of these strategies and tactics, one thing is for certain: the negotiations have not been satisfactory to either party. Both feel that they have given up too much already. Conciliation has given way to retaliation, real or perceived, and there is now considerable pressure for the negotiators to force the other party into submission. The final outcome is being escalated by political pressures faced by the Clinton administration and the new Japanese government led by Prime Minister Miyazawa.

The recent round of talks began in 1993 when the United States took a different and refreshing approach to the negotiations by focusing on establishing broad frameworks such as those discussed in Chapter 3. These frameworks would provide the overall objectives and would focus the parties on establishing goals at some point in the future which would ensure that the goals would be achieved. These frameworks were actually established in early 1993, and included the following understandings:

- Target five areas for trade expansion.
- Set a broad expectation for automobile exports.
- Establish guidelines for quotas on semiconductors.

Once these frameworks were established, the parties believed that it would be easier to then develop specific measures to determine compliance. This is exactly where the negotiations broke down. The U.S. negotiators did not adequately assess the unwillingness of the Japanese to negotiate rigid and specific goals which had to be adhered to. The Japanese did not realize the necessity to establish these targets or goals immediately nor could they predict the continual rise of the Japanese yen against the value of the dollar.

There were also numerous incorrect assumptions being made by both parties which lead to the creation of a climate of mistrust and uncertainty in the negotiations. Some of the potentially incorrect assumptions on the part of the U.S. and Japanese delegations include the following:

- Misjudgment about the real desires of either party to reach an agreement
- Long-term objectives of the parties in terms of market penetration
- The pressures being placed on the respective leaders of each country
- The true negotiating "face" being exhibited
- Looking at win/lose strategies as the compromise position to be taken
- Using a negotiation process which is acceptable to both parties

Before the parties can realistically *begin* meaningful discussions, they must first reach agreement on the basic facts which lie at the foundation of the negotiations. First, resolve the assumptions. It is much easier to work from the point where a win/win solution can be developed to match up with the facts, the strategies, the goals, and the expectations of the parties. This must be done in an environment of honesty. Then, it *can* happen. If the negotiators don't believe this simple premise, they must be replaced with people who do.

Politically, President Clinton was being chastised for letting the Japanese off the hook by not pressing for targets or quotas as a condition of the initial negotiations and the Japanese Prime Minister was being admonished for caving in to American pressure to resume the talks on establishing firm targets. Meanwhile, the chief U.S. negotiator, Mickey Kantor, was threatening retaliatory moves and the Clinton administration was encouraging the U.S. team to take an aggressive, noncompromising approach to the Japanese team. The Japanese then took an equally aggressive stance using words such as "countermeasures" and "retaliation" with increasing frequency. The talks appear to be steadfastly deadlocked at the time of this writing and no apparent, reasonable outcome is assured. What happened and what can we learn from the outcome of the negotiations?

One of the difficulties with managing these types of negotiations is the constantly changing influence of the press, political factions, and the personalities of the parties involved. Furthermore, the chief negotiators change every two years or so. There is absolutely no constancy of purpose or approach used. These are severe problems to be faced by any negotiator or negotiating team. But one wonders whether there has really been an effort to develop a plan and stick with it over a course of years. This must be done!

One approach that could be followed is to turn the whole process over to professional negotiators (such as foreign service officers) who would manage the long-term relationship with occasional fine-tuning and influence by the political leaders who change with elections over the years. The career people would provide desperately needed stability and continuity, and their contribution and expertise could be greatly valued and utilized by the politicians.

Iranian Hostages

In our view, the attempted negotiation for the release of the American hostages held by Iran was one of the most public negotiations ever. All one had to do was to turn on the television and see the pictures of the hostages and their immediate release became a national obsession. The Irangate proceedings and Oliver North's conviction will stand out as an example of a negotiating strategy gone wrong. Coupled with the failed attempt to rescue the hostages by the Carter administration, the chief question to be answered for those of us who evaluate negotiation outcomes, is: How did the U.S. get itself in a position where these options were *even attempted?*

Like the trade negotiations with Japan, these negotiations received an incredible amount of public interest, mostly because lives were at stake. Why weren't there more options to choose from? The answer, and the primary lesson learned, is that in order to negotiate, one must thoroughly understand the cultural context of the negotiators and the goals of the other party.

This learning is demonstrated by the utter failure of the U.S. and others to convince the Iranian leaders to release the hostages under any terms. We either needed to offer weapons or devise ways to literally take the hostages back unilaterally. One must only review excerpts from a cable sent by the chargé d'affaires of the U.S. Embassy in Teheran on August 13, 1979 to Cyrus R. Vance, then Secretary of State, to glean the key aspects of the Iranian perspective which were not addressed in the U.S. negotiation strategy. The cable asked Mr. Vance to carefully consider the special features of conducting negotiations in the Persian environment. The chargé d'affaires, L. Bruce Laingen, pointed to six lessons "for those who would negotiate" with individuals from Iran. These are as follows:

- One should never assume that his side of the issue will be recognized. The negotiator must force his position upon the other party.
- One should not expect the Iranians to perceive the advantages of a long-term relationship based on trust. The Iranian perspective is that negotiators should be adversaries.
- Interlocking relationships of all aspects of an issue must be painstakingly, forcefully, and repeatedly developed.
- One should insist on performance as the *sine qua non* at each stage of negotiations. Statements of intention count for almost nothing.
- Cultivation of good will for good will's sake is a waste of effort. Mutuality must be stressed.
- One should be prepared for the threat of breakdowns in the negotiation process at any given moment. It should be expected that the Iranian side will resist any form of rational negotiating process.

If you were one of the negotiators, what would your negotiation strategy be? How would you deal with the characteristics of negotiations described in this cable?

2.5 NEED FOR A PROCESS

The negotiating failures described up to this point all have one common feature: the unsuccessful party lacked a rational negotiation process. Without a defined process, there is always uncertainty about the reason(s) for results achieved.

So what is our process about? Why is it effective? What distinguishes it from approaches followed in the cases we have cited? Let us first describe it, then we will address these questions.

This process contains six distinguishable steps: Defining, planning, organizing, taking control, closing negotiations, and continuous improvement. Each step must be accomplished in order to produce optimal results. The flow of each of these steps is reflected in the rendition of the model displayed in Figure 2.1.

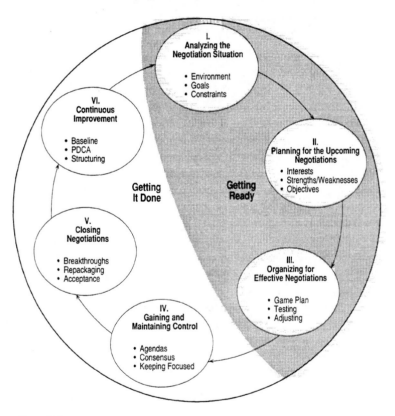

Figure 2.1:

Six Steps to Success

2.6 STEP 1: ANALYZING THE NEGOTIATION SITUATION: THE IMPORTANCE OF ISSUE DEFINITION AND ENVIRONMENTAL FACTORS

In the cases we cited above, it was clear that some of these steps were missing. For example, each negotiator would have benefited from a clear analysis of the real issues to be settled, as well as the environment surrounding the discussions.

Let's briefly examine the first step in our process, in which the negotiator defines what is to be negotiated. In order to do this, there are three specific tasks to be accomplished:

1. Examine the environment surrounding the negotiation.
2. Establish overall goals for the negotiation.
3. Identify any constraints which must be managed or allowed for.

To define the environment, a number of key aspects impacting the negotiating relationship should be identified. The history of previous negotiating encounters can be evaluated. Who won? Why? What happened after the negotiations? Have the negotiators changed? How would you characterize the quality of the negotiation sessions? Did the parties reach their goals? By answering these questions, you can get a "quick and dirty" picture about the emotional or personal "baggage" that the negotiators might be bringing to the negotiating table. The impact of these environmental factors can be best appreciated through illustration. Consider the following case study.

2.7 GE vs. UNIONS

During the 1950s, the General Electric Company experienced a prolonged period of unhappy labor relations. A series of lengthy, costly strikes was attributed to the combination of vocal aggressive unions and stern industrial relations policies advocated by the company. The architect of the General Electric negotiation policy, Director of Industrial Relations, George Boulware, became legendary for his negotiation style. The company approach would be to come up with its best offer at the very beginning of talks, announce that it would go no further and stand fast in that position. The result often was a very bitter standoff; raucous, sometimes violent strikes; and a harsh climate which pervaded the management/labor relationship. The idea of a win/win result, had they even heard of the term, would be the furthest thing from the minds of these negotiators. Anyone planning a negotiation between these parties should have considered the history of the relationship to develop objectives with some chance of amicable attainment.

2.8 REAGAN VS. PATCO

Another example of environmental factors occurred in the dispute between the federal government and the Air Traffic Controllers in 1981. After the Controllers' union, PATCO, went on strike, newly elected President Reagan invoked a long-standing federal law forbidding strikes against the government, and fired all the members of the striking union. The action stunned the controllers since the law had not been invoked in previous strikes by postal workers or other federal employees. The firing, which sent shockwaves throughout organized labor circles, won enthusiastic support for Reagan from business executives.

As a negotiations tactic, it proved a master stroke. In retrospect, even though it severely hampered air transportation, the firing was feasible for a number of reasons:

• The unions had been losing strength throughout the 1970s with membership at a new low.
• The public, after struggling along with inflation, unemployment, and high interest rates, was not very tolerant of strikes by public servants.
• Reagan had just won a landslide election and felt he had a mandate to take strong action.

In deciding to take this unprecedented action the White House would have concluded that the prevailing public mood would support such a move. In the negotiations environment that was created by Reagan's action, it would be a long time before government employees would strike again.

These are both large scale cases in which the environment was created by obvious factors such as public sentiment or well-known company/union relations. Similar environmental constraints, although less apparent, exist in the smallest negotiations, depending on factors such as market conditions, buyer/seller history, and personal background of the participants. Such influencing factors should be an important concern for anyone developing a negotiations plan.

Thus in Step 1, when broad goals for the negotiation are being determined, as well as the constraints that limit attainability of such goals, the planner must consider all of the background surrounding the issues to be resolved. The prevailing question should be: What can we accomplish and how far can we go, given the overall situation, history, and circumstance we and the opposition find ourselves in?

The goals should reflect the strategic needs of the negotiator, whether representing a firm, government, union, or the negotiator as an individual. The strategic needs are delineated in Step 1 and their relationship to individual objectives developed in Step 3.

2.9 STEP 2: PLANNING FOR THE UPCOMING NEGOTIATIONS: ESTABLISH COMMON OBJECTIVES FOR THE NEGOTIATIONS

Once the environment has been examined and responded to, the objectives of the upcoming negotiations should be established. These objectives should have a strategic flair to them, and although they could be quantitative in nature, the overall "framework" of the negotiations should be represented. These objectives provide the basis for reaching agreement with the other party on the following issues:

1. The structure of the negotiations
2. How the parties should "feel" once negotiations are completed
3. Duration
4. Participation
5. Responsibilities of the parties for data, note taking, leading sessions
6. The expected business, personal, or public results of the negotiations

Examples of these mutually shared objectives may provide even more definition of what we are envisioning here.

1. Structure   The negotiations will be accomplished by teams representing each party, each led and conducted by a designated leader.

2. Benefits   Both parties will reach their goals as fairly as possible.

3. Duration   The negotiations will be completed by June 30, 1995.

4. Responsibilities   Party A will be responsible for note taking and data accuracy while Party B will be responsible for all records and time keeping.

5. Participation   Representatives from both parties will participate equally in the negotiations, with each party willing to work together to achieve mutually satisfactory results.

6. Results   Party A will develop a long-term customer relationship with Party B where joint product development projects will be undertaken and the combined effort of both parties will make each party stronger as a separate enterprise.

These objectives envision a participative process with both parties sharing equally in the negotiations "work" and then both sharing equally in the results. Just reviewing the objectives can provide an overview of what the parties want from the negotiations process. Agreeing to them may establish a positive climate for the negotiations, thus enhancing prospects for success.

As in Step 1, where broad environmental effects are considered, here the negotiator must consider the particular interests of each party and their relative strengths and weaknesses. The aim is to develop objectives which reflect each party's concerns and to structure an agenda which provides for an orderly examination of the issues as well as a road map to their resolution. In Step 2, the strategic goals are converted into specific objectives to be attained in the negotiation, as part of building toward a detailed tactical plan, that is the product of Step 3.

2.10 STEP 3: ORGANIZING FOR EFFECTIVE NEGOTIATIONS

In Step 3 we conclude the process of detailed planning for the negotiator, building on the goals and objectives developed in Steps 1 and 2. The most important product of Step 3 is a game plan which lays out an agenda reflecting the relative importance of the issues and the order in which they will be discussed. It also involves techniques for testing and adjusting the plan prior to the actual beginning of negotiations. An important facet of Step 3 is keeping in proper perspective the strategic considerations so that long-term interests are not sacrificed in responding to short-term opportunities. Since strategic/tactical balance is crucial to the success of negotiations, these concepts are addressed extensively in this section.

2.11 STRATEGIC CONSIDERATIONS

Strategy is an overworked word in negotiations, being applied as it often is to every slight move or change in position that occurs as a negotiation runs its course. It would perhaps be helpful to consider the word in its classic sense. In military parlance, strategy is concerned with the big picture or the overall large-scale objective of a campaign. In World War II, the U.S. Pacific Theater strategy was to retake territory lost to Japan by invading only selected islands, and bypassing targets in between. The question of how particular territories would be assaulted, that is, whether by amphibious forces, airborne troops, or close support of troop landings by aircraft carriers, etc., were all tactical decisions, designed to carry out the grand strategy. In the European Theater the strategic debate was where a second front in Europe should be started.

The key point here is that strategic thinking had to be constant, and could only be changed if a cataclysmic event occurred. For example, the U.S. strategy for recapturing the Pacific was shaped by the

Pearl Harbor attack, the major defeat of the Japanese carrier force in the battle of Midway, the loss of the Philippines, etc. Although significant or newsworthy, a tactical development such as the prolonged battle for Guadalcanal did not alter the U.S. strategic goal. It may have affected changes in tactics—that is, techniques for carrying out the strategy—but the strategy itself did not change.

How might we apply this historic military logic to negotiations? The grand strategy concerns major objectives for, say, a firm, such as: reaching agreement on a new contract with a union, establishing a long-term relationship with a major supplier, gaining an important niche in a new market, acquiring rights to a new product line, or buying out a competitor to protect future markets. In a negotiation to achieve goals such as these it is important to stay focused on the major issue separating the parties. Side issues, compromising offers and their timing, and personalities of the participants are tactical matters which are critical to the attainment of the strategic goals but should not really alter the goals themselves.

Most successful negotiators are able to maintain focus and employ a longer term perspective on negotiations. This allows them to use a wide range of negotiation results in the short-term to achieve their long-term requirements. These individuals use flexible thinking in planning for achieving negotiation results. They ask "what if" questions and seek a range of outcomes over the short and medium terms. They might also challenge the status quo or precedent when pursuing their negotiation strategy.

In the cases we have described, the parties approached the negotiation problems from differing strategic perspectives. In its relations with Japan, the United States with its usual short-term focus was dealing with parties who traditionally take a longer view of things. MTI lost sight of its strategic objective because of an unexpected, probably short-term, change in their income position.

Strategic thinkers in negotiations are not only interested in the long-term but also wait for the right time and place to address particular issues. For instance, they would not identify their specific needs until after introductory meetings have been completed. They recognize that timing is critical (read essential) in achieving satisfactory negotiation results. Haven't you been pressured by someone at the wrong time to buy something, or agree with something, or accept something? You probably rejected them immediately, got angry, or asked them to ask you later. In any event, you most probably did not reach agreement! Details sometimes are thorns in the strategic thinker's feet. Too many specifics make it very difficult to see the end result, the long-term perspective. The car manufacturers negotiate with TV viewers when they advertise their closed-end leases or lease purchases. You probably have seen the commercials. They sell you on the car first then they hit you with the small print regarding the lease terms and conditions. It may be annoying but it is an effective way to do it! The real message here is: don't inundate the other party with details . . . select a few critical points and ensure they understand and agree with the most important ones.

In addition to maintaining long-term focus, good strategic thinkers never lose sight of the *controllable* aspects of negotiations. They attempt to be proactive in ensuring that they can influence these controllable factors to the greatest extent. Examples include the following:

- Location
- Agenda items
- Timing conflicts
- Members of the negotiation team
- Data to be shared
- Written communications
- Ethics and business practices
- Costs for negotiations (lost time)
- Number of negotiation sessions

Good negotiators recognize that by failing to control these factors they will probably fail to control the substantive issues. Often these items simply are not controlled at all and the negotiations drag on, seem endless, or cost the participants too much. Even worse, sometimes the other party manages to steer these procedural discussions, resulting in a less than satisfactory outcome for the party that had lost control. Effective strategic thinkers challenge the negotiation constraints presented by their own team or organization or by the other party. Challenging the very essence of the negotiable packages of options may result in innovative solutions not considered before: items like project budget, financial agreements, payment terms, project direction, key personnel, location of the work, and legal terms and conditions. These should be viewed as challenges to overcome rather than bona fide constraints which will be used to define the four walls of an agreement.

The process we have designed proposes a step-by-step discipline for conducting negotiations. The most critical stage of the process is planning, in which strategic and tactical approaches are developed to provide an integrated approach into a detailed game plan. The result is a balanced weighting of long- and short-term goals so that proper needs are given focus throughout the negotiations. With this approach, strategic thinking is easier to achieve.

Strategic thinkers also strive to integrate the views of the other negotiating party in their views, discussions and solutions. Failing to consider the other party, their views, and perhaps their organization may induce distrust, unbalanced interests, or quite simply biased or arbitrary alternatives. Strategic thinkers also balance the resources of people, money, and things by carefully drafting a number of short- and long-term solutions which satisfy both parties' interests. Once in negotiations, these alternatives can be evaluated for reasonableness and applicability.

A personal experience may illustrate the importance of strategic integration in negotiations. While at Prime Computer, Mr. Harris negotiated corporate-wide contracts with outside suppliers for the provision of computer peripherals such as disk drives, personal computers, and printers. In one particular negotiation, which lasted for two days, most parties believed that they had a reasonable deal. The discussions and agreements were hard fought, particularly in these areas:

- Pricing
- Warranty

- Service
- Training
- Engineering, changes
- Patent rights
- Applicable law
- Options
- Manuals

Both parties celebrated the completion of the contract with a dinner and good wishes. As is customary, the supplier representative, who was a Senior Vice President, left with the contract to be signed by an authorized representative of his company (the company secretary) and would then forward those contracts to Prime for signature. The signed copies of the contract were not forwarded promptly. When Mr. Harris followed up with this Senior Vice President he was told that upon further review, his "people" could not accept the terms. Upon further investigation, it was due to this individual's lack of communication with his home office. Consequently, he agreed to provisions which couldn't be supported by his company. He didn't receive appropriate input and feedback. The contract had to be completely renegotiated.

By the way, the Senior Vice President was never heard from again. . . .

2.12 WHY A STEP-BY-STEP PROCESS HELPS

We believe that following a logical step-by-step procedure is crucial to maintaining a proper balance between long-term and short-term considerations. In Step 1, the major strategic goals for the negotiations are decided along with reasonable assumptions of limits and constraints given the background of the negotiation issues(s) and any environmental concerns. In Step 2, the negotiator lays out the specific objectives to be achieved in light of particular strengths and weaknesses. Futhermore, in prioritizing the issues, consideration is given to mutuality of interests, in creating a structure in which a matrix of issues reflects their relative importance to the separate parties.

In Step 3, the negotiator develops a plan for tactical moves which are designed to achieve the strategic goals outlined in Step 1. By using the discrete steps, the negotiator is able to differentiate between strategy and tactics, thus maintaining a sound balance between long- and short-term interests.

2.13   THE CRUCIAL ROLE OF NEGOTIATION PLANNING

In our planning for this book, as well as in research to support our training practice, we wanted to test a belief that both of us held deeply: those who plan, or think strategically, prior to negotiation are more successful. We tested this belief by sending out a questionnaire asking respondents to tell us something about their successes and failures. In almost every case, we found that "successes" contained many elements of strategic thinking and planning, and "failures" lacked many of these elements. Here are examples of what we found:

Successes: Preparation and setting clear objectives and trade-off alternatives were advantageous in repricing a new product, achieving a target price asked by customers.

Team participation in the formation of a prenegotiation plan between a buyer and a seller, and careful attention to a "partnership" oriented approach contributed to a successful manufacturing license relationship.

Preparation and knowledge of past relations and purchase history contributed to the achievement of a successful three-year purchase agreement.

Failures: Lack of preparation and planning caused an expensive last-time purchase of an important component.

Lack of a team approach, with individuals sharing their own personal interests, squashed a number of particularly lucrative new business partnerships.

Arbitrary setting of targets to be achieved by different departments greatly influenced the loss of a high-quality supplier.

We could all add more, perhaps better, examples of situations where the lack of strategic negotiation thinking caused poor results. Let's reverse the trend . . . let's plan . . . let's keep our strategic goals uppermost in our minds . . . and let's work with the other party to see how our mutual goals can be met, as indicated in Figure 2.2.

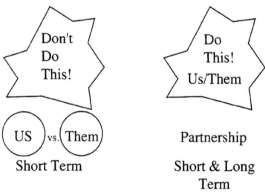

Figure 2.2

Balancing short- and Long-Term Needs

Once you have completed these three steps, you are now prepared for conducting the upcoming negotiations.

2.14 STEP 4: GAINING AND TAKING CONTROL

The premise of our fourth step is that if you don't want to waste all the efforts you have put forth in the Getting Ready phase, you must be sure that you implement what you have planned for. This is easier said than done, because planning naturally happens based on past experience and the expectations of the parties, not on real-time feedback received, for example, in a negotiation session. This step is consequently very critical in assuring that you receive the return on investment from the planning phase. All of the previous work—strategic analysis, goal setting, objectives definition, game plan development—has served to create an orderly plan to enter a negotiation, establish control, and maintain the momentum. There are a number of simple techniques to aid you in gaining control of the negotiations process, and then keeping control to the conclusion of the process.

Agendas are the product of Step 3 and are used to focus the discussions between the parties. Normally jointly developed, they include a list of points to be discussed in a given negotiations session, with time allocation assigned. Both time frames and points for discussion are tightly monitored so that individual sessions achieve expectations.

The techniques of reaching *consensus* can be used to build the oppositions's acceptance regarding not only the negotiating flow but also the solutions and agreements reached. This technique is extremely powerful because it eliminates all but the leading, indisputable alternative and thus gets the backing of those involved. Consensus provides not only a way to gain agreement, but it also focuses the parties toward a few, well-documented alternatives. Once an alternative receives team endorsement, it's really impossible to move into other less deserving areas.

"Keeping focused" should be the motto of the negotiator in the 1990s. Climbing the Tom Peters bandwagon on this one is crucial. Focus is critical to maintaining proper perspective on long-vs. short-term objectives. Stick to your plan, unless it fails miserably or if circumstances (like technology, political shifts, etc.) dictate. Work with the other party to keep focused on what you set out to do. It should be noted, however, that the plan is the product of your own thinking and should be updated as reactions from the opposition are received.

This is clearly not the case when there is a hostile takeover of a company. These types of situations occur all the time. The story of the bid for Lockheed by Northrop was well documented in 1994. Lockheed management was vehemently against the merger due to perceived differences in managerial philosophy between the companies. Ultimately, Martin Marietta became the "White Knight" and purchased the company. In these circumstances, one does wonder whether the company that is being taken over actually loses out as a result of accepting a White Knight's offer. The acquiring company generally pays more for the company and has a higher debt load.

People encounter these types of circumstances every day; the parties with which we wish to negotiate may not share the same sense of urgency or priority and yet we may be forced to work out a negotiated settlement with them. They don't have the luxury of a "White Knight" appearing to save the day. You are faced with the task of working with the other party and jointly reaching agreement. Focus, consensus, and use of agendas can help in overcoming barriers and obstacles in negotiations, particularly when faced with these types of dilemmas.

2.15 STEP 5: CLOSING NEGOTIATIONS

One of the authors' sons is an effective negotiator. He always asks, "What's in it for me?" This may sound egotistical or selfish, but in a way, he is right. In negotiations, everyone needs to get something they want. In the process of closing negotiations, then, each party must answer this question in some shape or form.

- Is it what I wanted?
- Did I get less than the other party?
- Who won?
- Could I get more?

A question we believe should be asked at this juncture is: Does the package of alternatives most appealing to me satisfy my objectives? More often than not, parties come into a negotiation with only *one* alternative for discussion. If the parties' respective *"one"* solutions do not intersect or complement each other, the chances of both parties being satisfied are almost nonexistent.

We believe it to be important for negotiators to develop a number of alternatives for acceptable solutions to the negotiation. *Brainstorming* is an excellent technique for developing options, and subjecting them to objective evaluation before accepting or discarding them. This is done by considering each available option, testing it for reasonableness, then finding ways to group different options together to add up to packages of value or "packaged" solutions. Consider the way that personal computers or automobiles are "packaged" with various options, and you note the result: The buyer gets a computer or car with the features they want. Two people can buy a car from the same dealer, and both will have differing levels of satisfaction with the negotiations.

Use this approach when developing packages for discussion. Ask the other party what packages of options will satisfy their needs. Chances are that both of you will have considered the same packages so agreement is then possible. Acceptance is greater when the parties can structure the results jointly and honestly.

We encourage negotiators in this step to find *breakthroughs*— those issues, events, tactics, concepts, people, or appropriate times which can jump-start or otherwise compel the parties to reach an agreement. Examples of these types of breakthroughs abound:

- Change of negotiator
- Press for agreement before end of quarter
- Major success of new product
- Higher profits achieved than expected
- Lower profits achieved
- Recognition by trade organization
- Problems cited with products or services

- Promotions or setbacks
- Announced layoffs

All of these events or circumstances introduce an aspect of change into negotiations. Change allows people to think differently about things. It makes sense to take advantage "of the moment" to attempt to reach agreement.

Let's examine a number of these changes. When a company is downsizing its work force, it normally asks its employees to consider early retirement on a voluntary basis. Terms are normally spelled out well in advance and the respective parties choose the best option for them. In the case of layoffs at General Electric, IBM, and other major companies, those individuals make the choice knowing full well that if they choose not to take early retirement, they might be ultimately laid off without the benefits originally offered. The risks of not choosing the right options is the impetus needed to maximize the number of early retirements, which avoids the more emotional layoff decision making.

For example, when a company has an exclusive new product, it can command a higher margin for its products.

You can look at the three aspects of this step toward closure—acceptance, breakthroughs, and packaging—as follows in Figure 2.3.

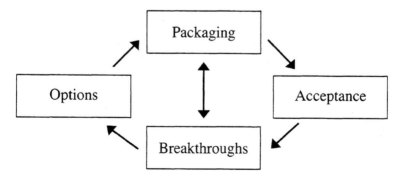

Figure 2.3

Closing the Negotiations Process Flow

The point is to find ways and times to reach agreement which are non-traditional, unique, innovative, and mutually satisfactory. Try it!

2.16 STEP 6: CONTINUOUS IMPROVEMENT

The only way to improve is to evaluate performance, determine the gaps in between what you expected and what you achieved, and then develop an action plan to improve performance. There are many existing templates or models which focus the negotiator on continuous improvement.

You first must have a baseline of information. What went well? What went wrong? Were there any surprises? Were both parties' objectives satisfied? Where were the shortcomings and the gains? You can measure your performance by reviewing your objectives and determining the level of compliance. You can also review the steps in the negotiation process and determine in which steps you were most and least successful. Perhaps you didn't research the other party well enough, or used the wrong tactics or employed an awkward style. Perhaps the other party was more prepared than you were . . . and how did that affect the outcome? Introspection is an important element in improving negotiation skills since it provides a baseline for improved performance.

Once you diagnose where you were unsuccessful, then you should devise a way to try other alternatives in the next negotiations. The Plan-Do-Check-Act cycle, to be explained later, takes this plan (Do), asks you to evaluate performance, and then asks whether or not you wish to standardize the approach, try it again, or scrub it for another alternative (Act). This process is graphically displayed in Figure 2.4.

As you can see, it also includes a loop back to "plan." This is also important as it emphasizes a constant analysis, evaluation, and assessment of performance so that negotiation skills can be optimized. Everyone can still learn to negotiate better. The core of the Deming philosophy as adopted in Japan (and now in the U.S.) is that improvement is always possible, so we must seek continuous improvement.

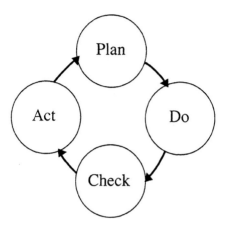

Figure 2.4

The Plan-Do-Check-Act Cycle

This contrasts with the prevalent Western idea that once we improve a product we stop working on it to sell as fast and for as long as we can. If we apply the Deming idea to negotiation we never rest on our laurels but endeavor to see how we could have done better.

Lastly, structuring the next steps after completion of the negotiation is the final aspect of this step. What do you standardize? What do you improve upon next? What gaps can be addressed? What do your fellow negotiators want? Structuring is like putting together an action plan . . . which allows you to lay out the tasks for improvement, and reap the benefits.

Consider a number of the excellent negotiators—Kissinger, Iacocca, Uberoth, Welch;—they all try to improve their performance in negotiations over time. They employ the PDCA process intuitively. They studied themselves, the process used, the results, and the problems encountered. They worked to close gaps in performance and devised ways to improve the next time around.

Kissinger gave equal weight to preparation and execution. Welch takes a financial and market-share perspective with his approach. Iacocca built consensus and support from lawyers and the average American. Uberroth convinced corporate sponsors that supporting the L.A. Olympics would not only be a public service but was also good business. These individuals, over their long careers, thought long and hard about what they wanted, as well as the needs of the other party, and applied the learning from previous negotiations. They strove to do better every time they negotiated!

Getting Ready: Analyzing the Negotiation Situation

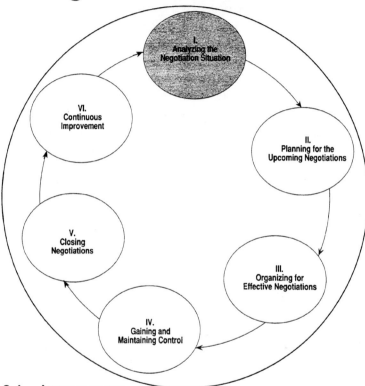

3.1 INTRODUCTION

Perhaps the most critical factor in negotiation success is the participants' clear awareness of what is to be achieved. Many students of management science would agree that the first step in problem solving is a clear definition of the problem. Continuous improvement teams routinely begin their activities with a free discussion of the problems to be targeted and then reach agreement on the scope of the improvement effort.

Negotiation is fundamentally a technique of problem solving. The chances for successful conclusion to a negotiation effort are greatly enhanced if the participants have a clear understanding of the problem to be solved—i.e., the issue(s) that separate them from reaching agreement. In this chapter we underscore the importance of defining and scoping what is to be negotiated, and the factors influencing that process.

3.2   CONSIDERING THE NEGOTIATION ENVIRONMENT

Fundamental to any successful negotiation is a plan. An obvious comparison is the need for a sailor leaving port to have some specific idea of what route to follow to reach a particular destination. In laying out such a plan, the mariner must consider the state of the waters to be traveled and the problems and obstacles that are likely to be confronted. On this rough foundation he can begin to develop a detailed plan to achieve his goals.

Like the sailor laying out a course, the effective negotiator begins his planning by considering the rough outlines of the negotiation situation:

- What am I trying to achieve?
- What is the environment in which I must operate?
- What problems am I likely to encounter?

Let's apply these questions to a rather common situation: the purchase of a house. First, what is the buyer trying to achieve? Most of the time, the objective is a decent home at a fair price that will satisfy family needs. Sometimes, the property is being purchased as an investment opportunity. These differing needs will naturally shape the motivation, flexibility (or lack thereof) and emotional commitment of the buyer in any negotiation with a prospective seller. In either case, the size of the house and the range of acceptable prices will be pivotal factors in the first attempts to reach agreement.

Secondly, what is the state of the environment in which the buyer must operate? Is it a buyer's or seller's market in the particular area? What is the current state of financial markets, as affecting mortgage rates? Is the market relatively dead or lively? Is the target community experiencing growth or decline? Is there a shortage, or a glut, of desirable properties on the market? If the buyer has children, what is the reputation of schools in the community? (This factor is important also to childless buyers, because it affects property values.) What recreational, cultural, and social opportunities exist? Are there a number of organized brokers serving the area, or is real estate business conducted at a less formal personal level by principals concerned?

Thirdly, what problems are likely to emerge? Do I foresee any personal credit problems, and/or are local banks generally reluctant to extend credit. What about regulatory problems with local governments such as water and sewage constraints, lead paint, and asbestos concerns? To what extent can the buyer lay these back on the seller? Is the seller likely to renege on commitments regarding terms of sale and post-sale defects, and how can the buyer ensure protection against such happenings?

The development of such a list of concerns and questions is not difficult for a matter as complex, or so personally significant, as the purchase of a residence. The point of this book, however, is that every negotiation situation, no matter how simple, deserves similar scrutiny before discussion. For example, prior to a simple telephone call to reach agreement on a matter in dispute, such as a price check, or an alternative approach, it would behoove the party making the call to consider the objectives, the probable response of the other party, and the caller's response to any counter suggestion received. At the least, a list of "what ifs" should be developed. Underlying these questions is a concern for the environment in which the call is to be made and the ambient factors affecting both the caller and the other party. What time of the day or week is it? Is this a good time to call, etc.? If the matter is very simple and involves another party well known to the caller, then a mental list would perhaps suffice. The point is, *think before you speak*. Think about what is to be said to bring the elements of sound planning to the simplest negotiation.

In the mid 1980s, AMC (now Chrysler) had tried for years to negotiate with the Chinese government regarding agreement on establishing an assembly plant for their Jeep products. Initially, great progress was made as both parties established labor potential and logistics requirements. When it came down to negotiating the terms and conditions of the contract, negotiations came to a screeching halt due to disagreement as to what "acts of God" were. Normally understood by negotiators in western countries as circumstances arising out of such things as floods, hurricanes, and even labor strikes, the Chinese took offense to the notion that an act of God was negative and influential on a contract situation.

The summary point about the environment is that negotiations are never conducted in a vacuum. Each party's performance will be influenced by many factors beyond their control. The list is exhaustive: fiscal schedules, business needs, market conditions, personal distractions, public interest (especially in high visibility matters such as sports and entertainment negotiations, international disputes, govenmental policy, large–scale strikes, etc.), and proceedings of crucial personal importance to the participants. Within this high pressure arena of conflicting demands it is difficult for negotiators to remain focused on their primary objective, and sound planning must include detailed analysis to allow for the impact of such factors in developing a comprehensive, flexible approach to the negotiations at hand.

This analysis can be facilitated using a form of the type indicated in Figure 3.1 to guide you. Once completed, the form reveals the implications of the existing environment on upcoming negotiations.

This form also includes space for the would-be negotiator to develop an action plan to counteract environments characterized as "guarded" and "unfavorable." It should be noted, however, that the form permits consideration of circumstances characterized as excellent or good, so that the prospects for a favorable outcome are enhanced.

To further facilitate analysis of factors, conditions, and circumstances affecting a negotiation, the following is a list of items that might influence various kinds of negotiations. This list is not all-inclusive and the reader may very well come up with many more.

1. Subject matter of negotiations: _____

2. Date(s) to be scheduled: _____

	Yes	No
3. Negotiators on their side	Previously involved/known: ___	___
	___	___
	___	___
4. Negotiators on our side	Previously involved/known to other party ___	___
	___	___
	___	___

5. Previous negotiations on similar/identical topics

Subject Matter	Rating 1-5	Results	Acceptability Rating 1-5
1. ___	___	1. ___	1. ___
2. ___	___	2. ___	2. ___
3. ___	___	3. ___	3. ___

6. Our view of their viewpoints/interests _____

7. Their view of our viewpoints/interests _____

Implications _____

Figure 3.1

Negotiation Planning Form

8. Overall analysis of the negotiating environment

	Implications	Actions Required to Counteract
Excellent; favorable to both parties		
Very Good; steps have been taken to ensure open and amicable exchange		
Guarded; new players and new perspectives cause parties to take "wait and see" approach		
Unfavorable; past negotiations with other party produced unfavorable, even hostile viewpoints		

Figure 3.1

Negotiation Planning Form

Continued

3.3 BUSINESS-TO-BUSINESS NEGOTIATIONS:

Market Conditions	Labor Relations/History	Inflation Factors
Economic Situation	Existing Labor Contracts	Prevailing Rental Rates
Interest Rates	Available Capacity	Zoning Laws
Long-Range Company Plans	Local Labor Availability	Tooling Ownership
Market Strategy	Investment Strategy	Patent, Proprietary Rights
Political Climate	Capitalization Policy	Built-in Wage Increases
Public Relations Concerns	Community Relations	

3.4 PERSONAL NEGOTIATION:

Interest Rates	Income Requirements	Family Space Needs
Market Conditions	Relocation Flexibility	Inflation Factors
Marital Situation	Cultural/Political Factors	Health Considerations
Local Property Values	Affordability	Climate Preferences
Auto Production Cycles	Education, Retirement Plans	Retirement, Health, Life Insurance
Seller's Business Needs		

3.5 GOVERNMENT-TO-GOVERNMENT:

Existing or Projected Treaties /Alliances	Political Situation	Timing re: Political Changes (elections, powershifts)
Military Strength	Currency Valuation	
Exchange Rates	Trade Policy and History	
Cultural Differences	Import/Export Balance	Historic Precedent

The effects of negotiation can have long lasting implications if they significantly impact the personal well-being of the participants. A recent story reported in the national press describes the negative views of Donald Douglas, Jr., head of one of the founding families of McDonnell-Douglas, regarding merger negotiations which took place in 1967. At the time of the merger, Douglas Aircraft, a pioneer of early aircraft which made it economical for the general public to fly, had made some risky investments which had gone sour. It was forced to combine with another company to avoid a financial crash.

When the merger was announced in 1967, Donald Douglas further assured all employees of excellent lifetime pension and health benefits for themselves as well as their spouses. In 1994, McDonnell-Douglas executives now wish to terminate those benefits. Lost, in the apparently hasty negotiations which accompanied the merger, was the redemption by Douglas of what they actually lost in the deal . . . their identity, values, and their influence. Perhaps if they had evaluated the other more carefully, the results would have been better understood and longer lasting.

3.6   STRATEGIC CONCERNS

It is in this first step that strategic considerations must be weighed. After assessing the surrounding environment, the negotiator must begin to focus in on the goals to be attained in the upcoming session. At this point the goals are global (in the sense that they affect in a major way the world in which the negotiator lives) and of strategic significance. They could involve the way a company does business, a shift in product emphasis or huge growth in market share, or a major acquisition. On a smaller plane, it could involve a new residence for a family, a divorce settlement or a mortgage adjustment—all issues not earthshaking, but profoundly affecting the lives of the individuals involved.

The needs considered in Step 1 are those which dominate the concern of the participants and it is on their loss or attainment that the success of the negotiation will eventually be judged. In this phase of getting ready, the negotiator must consider any constraints that will put limits on attainment of major goals. Then, in follow-up planning, a game plan will be developed concerning the number of issues to be discussed, and their effect on the attainment of the major goals underlying the dispute to be settled.

3.7 DETERMINING NEEDS

As a starting point, the negotiator must focus on the specific needs to be satisfied by the upcoming negotiation. Whatever issue is to be decided, the negotiator must determine what particular needs must be met if the session is to be considered a success. It is important to note that a "need" is something that must be had, as opposed to a "want," which connotes an element of "nice to have."

In scoping the negotiation problem, the planner must define what is needed, while deciding which of the number of needs is short-term vs. long-term, as well as whether an issue is "must-have" that serves as the building block for the negotiation plan.

Let's look at a celebrated public example. In the summer of 1994, the major league baseball owners were considering a new contract with the players' association. The primary issue was whether a salary cap should be agreed upon. To explain briefly, some background might be helpful. In the 1970s, Curt Flood, a center-fielder for the Saint Louis Cardinals, challenged the legality of the contract he had with his employer. His suit eventually reached the Supreme Court, which decided that the existing contract arrangements, which provided exclusive first-refusal rights to a player's services forever, were unconstitutional. After this major victory for all professional athletes, players were free at the end of their contracts to sell their services to any club owner. Previously, if a player did not agree to terms offered by a team he had once contracted with, he had no choice but to accept the offer or retire.

The result of this decision was widespread bidding for players who were now free agents. Salaries escalated alarmingly and the old established order crumbled. Wealthy clubs—or those in lucrative markets—easily contracted with the best players. To put a ceiling on skyrocketing costs, owners were attempting to establish a salary cap. In developing their budget, clubs would pay no more than a specific league-established ceiling in filling their rosters. All clubs would agree to the salary cap figure, which could be adjusted from time to time.

As the negotiations approached, the primary question was if the owners' regarded the attainment of a salary cap as a must-have. Could they continue to operate without one? As for the players, did they have to obtain a contract which would not put a ceiling on their compensation potential? For each party, the issue could become a basic need. In the ultimate negotiations, the seriousness of the issue would be reflected in their willingness to call for a strike, or a lock-out, should the issue not be resolved. A mid-summer interruption would be a serious blow to baseball in the national consciousness—but its occurrence would signal the gravity with which both parties viewed the salary cap issue.

The salary cap issue is an example of a need. In determining its position on a possible agenda, the negotiator would perhaps use it as a must-have. On the other hand it could represent an issue which neither side would wish to resolve if that decision produced unacceptable consequences such as a mid-summer shutdown. It would be prudent, therefore, for negotiators on both sides to consider less portentous issues which could be used to break deadlocks and present some image of goodwill with the watching public.

Thus the negotiator must consider a number of needs, so that the unresolvable issue is not the only thing to be discussed but is considered only as part of a matrix of needs within which trade-offs can be made and a comprehensive agreement reached. Secondary issues also serve to provide fodder for the bargaining table, on which some time can be spent, while more serious issues are discussed away from the limelight, reducing public pressure on the negotiators.

3.8 PRIORITIES

In determining the needs of a particular case the negotiator must not only isolate those things to be attained but must prioritize them. Prioritization is necessary to lend some order to the planning; in fact, it would be impossible to schedule an order of discussion without some sense of the relative weight of issues. Which issues should be discussed first and which saved for a climactic session are important questions for the planner to consider.

Let's try a brief exercise in prioritization using the baseball negotiation example. The following is a list of possible issues that the management/union could discuss:

- Establishment of a ceiling for total salaries for each baseball club or a salary cap system
- Movement of any free agents (players) to highest bidder without the current owner receiving compensation from the player's new employer
- Owners' payment of larger share of retirement funding
- Payment of premiums for disability insurance
- Compensation for services during non-league games, such as spring training
- Community service required of players, without compensation, as a condition of employment
- Contributions by employers to charities in player's name and assignment of tax deductible credit
- Meal allowances, scheduling conveniences, and other work rules
- Individual performance incentives on which players' salaries could be based

You may be able to think of many other issues which could be added to the list.

After considering the list how would you rate the relative importance of each issue? Did you observe that the priorities differ, depending on which side of this controversy you are on? What is important to note is that each side must establish priorities. If each side sees the weight of each issue differently, there may be some difficulty in developing an agenda. The scheduling of issues could become an issue. The successful negotiator, therefore, will begin to exercise control immediately but not in such a way as to discourage the chances of reaching ultimate agreement.

Prioritization helps us decide which issues are "must haves," which can be used as give-aways, and which can be combined in a package to break an impasse. Prioritization thus helps in developing solutions to the mutual benefit of both parties.

Another important function of prioritization is its role in making participants see the importance of win/win negotiating. If an issue is recognized as a must-have to both parties, then extraordinary efforts must be made to create solutions which avoid the total loss on this vital point by either party. Otherwise, negotiations will reach a stalemate and ultimately fail. This recognition is the first step in the process of seeking solutions which both sides will judge, if not to be totally satisfactory, at least acceptable.

3.9 IDENTIFYING CONSTRAINTS

The process of determining needs is affected by many factors, not the least of which is a frank appraisal of the negotiation issues and their place in the participant's overall scheme of things. As described in the discussion of priorities, the negotiator must make a candid assessment of the relative criticality of each issue before placing it on a matrix of items to be settled. Honest objectivity is similarly required in identifying constraints. One must realize the limits to what can be realistically accomplished considering the position and probable attitude of the other party. In other words, just how much can the other party give? Conversely, just how much can you yield to accommodate his position? The answers to these questions establish the limits around each issue and help to build the framework for concessions.

Obviously, the negotiator is most familiar with the constraints that exist for his or her own position. Constraints arise from real barriers to flexibility, such as company policy, affordable mortgage payments, available liquid assets, production schedules, material lead times, existing legal agreements, etc.

The negotiator is less familiar with similar constraints that exist for the other party. During the planning stage the negotiator must gauge the level of flexibility open to the opposition. Prior to the actual discussion, such assessments are imperfect at best, but must be done to begin to structure a possible solution to the problem in dispute. Once the sessions begin, real learning commences and the negotiator will be able to judge the correctness of assumptions made. At that point the negotiation plan must be updated, and if necessary, the goals re-established.

The prudent negotiator must establish objectives that are *reasonable*. Now, "reasonable" is a word that some consider a cop-out, used by people unable to come up with hard, concrete descriptions, or fixed prices, or black-and-white answers. In legal circles, people are often held to a standard of reasonable performance, for example, in the case where one must make a *reasonable* effort (lawyers call it "due diligence") to provide security for customers/visitors or be held liable for injuries incurred by such persons on one's premises. We are told that a buyer should expect to pay a *reasonable* price—whatever that means. One definition is: the price that an objective third party would pay in the given circumstances. Some would say a reasonable price is whatever the market will bear. The federal government takes the position that a fair and reasonable price is assumed to result from an "adequate competition." Adequate competition is deemed to exist when qualified, competent bidders bid independently on essentially the same thing. Each of these defining terms is subject to some interpretation.

The term reasonable thus appears to have as many meanings as there are people doing the defining. For our purposes, in discussing negotiation objectives, the word *reasonable* means *attainable* by a negotiator acting in good faith with due consideration for the long- and short-term needs of his/her business, institution, family, union, or whatever interest is being represented.

"Reasonable" results can often be defined only in personal terms. What is reasonable to me may be outlandish to you. It's all a matter of appreciation and degree of comfort. It is also due to the extent to which negotiators have persuaded the other party, or are influenced by external factors, management or peer pressure, and to the amount of expediency actually included in the negotiation process.

Finally, let's discuss balancing objectives. The extreme and almost unending focus on short-term needs often overwhelms the negotiators on both sides and typically results in compromised results either in relation to long-term needs or as a function of established objectives. American society is very short-term focused. We want the income and the material things now. CEOs want to maximize this quarter's income. Professional sports teams succumb to fielding a magical aging team rather than rebuilding it with talented, young players. This causes us, as negotiators, to focus on short-term outcomes rather than long-term results.

The following principles apply in determining the reasonableness of objectives:

- The objective should be something that we have some real chance of attaining.
- The objective should be established in terms of what we will finally achieve and should not preclude starting with an initial offering from which we might have to yield.
- We must consider the other party's likely response—after all, he has "reasonable" objectives of his own.
- While we should be realistic as to what is attainable and should not aim too high, we should definitely not aim too low
- The negotiator should be guided at all times with the responsibility for making his or her best professional effort to attain the needed goals developed in the planning. He or she should be neither too hard nor too soft in the negotiation process, but must do whatever it takes to be successful, in every sense of the term.
- Finally, no one wishes to be termed unreasonable—thus the need for establishing reasonable objectives and acting reasonably in attempting to reach them.

Once these factors are taken into consideration, a carefully structured plan can be put into place for use in the upcoming negotiations. That is the subject of the next chapter.

Getting Ready: Planning for the Upcoming Negotiations

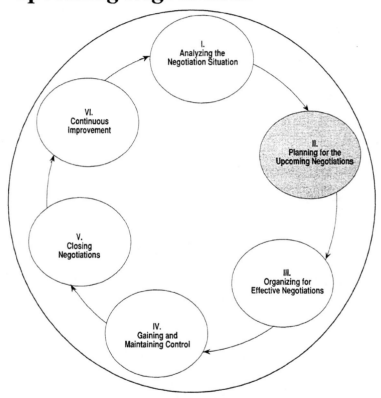

I.
Analyzing the
Negotiation Situation

VI.
Continuous
Improvement

II.
Planning for the
Upcoming Negotiations

V.
Closing
Negotiations

III.
Organizing for
Effective Negotiations

IV.
Gaining and
Maintaining Control

If you are like most negotiators we know, you feel you are too busy or lack the time to plan adequately for the upcoming negotiations. Yet you also probably realize that proper planning is one of the most critical pre-negotiation activities. Inadequate preparation or planning leads to setting unreasonable objectives, using inappropriate styles and tactics, and more importantly, it leads to the negotiator believing at the end of a series of negotiation events that goals were not satisfactorily met. This is primarily due to the unreasonable nature of the established objectives and the fact that unplanned negotiations are quick and somewhat uncontrolled.

Planning for an upcoming event always increases the probability for success. Examples of effective planning that have lead to exceptional results abound:

- Used by many companies implementing total quality management (TQM), Shewhart's continuous improvement process begins with the planning step. In his Plan-Do-Check-Act (PDCA) process, planning includes evaluating the current problem or situation, deciding why a particular practice or process should be improved, understanding the causes of the problem, and developing solutions to eliminate causes. This tool is used by individuals in problem solving situations in many corporations today. What would you "do" in the PDCA model without an adequate plan?
- The United States' incredible victory in the 1990 Gulf War was due to an equally incredible plan of troop deployment and coordination. It is already being heralded as one of the best planned military operations in modern times. Even though you would expect the military to create a "battle plan," why not use the "game plan" approach to derive goals, objectives, and strategies for the upcoming negotiations?
- Henry Kissinger, best known for his excellent negotiation work in the Egypt-Israel Camp David Peace Accord, considered planning and preparation to be his keys to success, stating that he allotted 50% of his negotiation time to planning activities.

Planning ensures that the negotiator anticipates what is to happen, knows approximately what the other party is going to propose, and establishes appropriate objectives and strategies. Planning will prepare the negotiator to face known issues during negotiations, thereby reducing the number of surprises encountered.

In general, planning issues include the following elements, also indicated in Figure 4.1.

- Goals—Broad statements of purpose, interest, and strategic intent
- Objectives—Specific measurable statements of what is to be derived from the negotiations
- Game Plan—Tangible planning to accomplish the objectives for the negotiation including schedules, styles, tactics, and makeup of the negotiation team
- Tools—Methods and processes which will be used to ensure the smooth implementation of the strategic plan, consisting of items such as consensus, collaboration, and control points

The primary function of Step 2 is the development of detailed plans for including the goals established in Step 1. Let us place this in context by revisiting the process of goal setting described in Step 1.

Figure 4.1

Elements of Negotiation Planning

4.1   ESTABLISHING GOALS

In the context of negotiations, goals are the broad statements of purpose. Developed through discussions with those individuals who represent the negotiator's constituency or simply his/her stakeholders, goals reflect the interests of the parties to the negotiations. Goals should be prepared in a clear and concise fashion so that they can be presented to the other side for comment and revision.

Examples would include:

- Enter into a new market
- Change the way we do business
- Reduce transaction costs
- Gain access to new technology

The goal of the United States when negotiating the 1994 General Agreement on Tariffs and Trade (GATT) was to create economic growth and good-paying jobs for Americans. It took over eight years across three presidential administrations for the negotiations to have developed an acceptable package for Congressional approval. The negotiating team used the broad goals to set objectives for the various industries involved such as steel, computer, aviation, agriculture, audio-visual, chemicals, electronics, pharmaceuticals, services, and textiles. Once the terms of the agreement were negotiated, the process was not complete. Since there were opponents to the agreement the Clinton Administration needed to negotiate with individual factions to gain broader acceptance. It cut deals with the steel, textile, and agriculture industries. It had to replace the revenue lost due to reduced tariffs so it worked with the House of Representatives to attach certain revenue-generating provisions to the agreement. Goals turning into objectives coupled with strategy; that's what the Clinton Administration and its negotiators acted on and implemented to deliver a package which purportedly will earn Americans over 122 billion dollars over a ten year period.

Note that goals do not include specific quantitative targets, as this will be the purpose of the objectives that follow. Goals provide the framework for the negotiations . . . they provide the scope of items to be discussed, and in essence, set the boundaries for the discussion. The procedures to follow for the framework are indicated in Figure 4.2.

Goal Setting Procedures:

- Define the overall goals for an upcoming negotiation from your perspective.

- Use three or four broad statements.

- Review these statements with the other party.

- Compare and contrast them.

- Try to reach agreement with the other party on the three to four goals
to be pursued.

- Restate the goals, gain agreement, and finalize the list by signing a document
memorializing the agreement.

Figure 4.2

Goal Setting Procedures

If you have done this, you have established common goals of the
parties. Now you must translate these goals into specific objectives.
But first let's apply what we've learned about setting goals.

4.2 Example/Application

The American-Japan trade talks have been ongoing for the last
20 years, with the negotiations ending in the establishment of quotas,
penalties, and negativism. These results were primarily due to both
parties taking aggressive bargaining approaches since neither side
wanted to "lose face" or give the impression that they were making
too many concessions. In administering the agreement, both parties
used threats to force each other to comply. In deep contrast to this
historical trend, however, the trade agreement reached by the representatives in 1993 resulted from the parties taking a completely different tack. "Frameworks" or broad statements of goals were used to
establish the boundaries for the negotiations. Establishing frameworks
allowed the participants to approach topics such as opening the
Japanese market for five types of American products and establishing
a potential for firm targets to be set at some point in the future.

4.3   EXERCISE

Let's apply the concepts of frameworks to an upcoming negotiation of yours. Complete the matrix described in Figure 4.3 in the areas provided.

Building a Framework

Negotiation Issue: _____

Your Goals: _____
_____

Other Parties' Goals: _____
_____

Similar Goals: _____
_____

Different Goals: _____
_____

Ideas to Combine _____
Different Goals: _____

Initial Set of   1. _____
Framework Items: 2. _____
                        3. _____
                        4. _____

Figure 4.3

Building a Framework Document

In developing a successful framework, the differing goals of the parties must be carefully combined in a way which satisfies the needs and goals of each party. This will probably require considerable negotiation between the parties, exchanging divergent viewpoints, and a joint resolve to reach agreement. Reaching agreement on a mutually agreeable goal in this manner might sound naive . . . but it can work if you and the other party want to reach eventual agreement.

4.4　ESTABLISHING OBJECTIVES

Once goals are developed, the parties can establish negotiation objectives which ensure that their own business, functional, and personal needs can be obtained. Objectives are specific statements of interests created by each party. They have the following characteristics:
- Quantitative
- Measurable
- Time-Specific
- Action-Oriented

To illustrate, let's look at some examples of goals and associated objectives. Consider the following:
- Goal: Enter into a new market.
  Objective: Reach 5% of market share within 24 months.
- Goal: Change the way we do business.
  Objective: Reduce the number of procedures by 25%.
- Goal: Reduce transaction costs.
  Objective: Employ computer-to-computer linkages for 40% of purchases.
- Goal: Gain access to new technology.
  Objective: Have systems in place by January 1st.

The idea here is for both parties to develop their own quantifiable objectives which fulfill the broad goals that we discussed. Then it is the joint responsibility of the parties to work together to achieve these objectives.

Objectives should be aligned with the goals established in the framework and at the same time, satisfy those business desires of the parties. A handy way to define those critical business desires is to brainstorm with the help of others about the mandatory business requirements to be obtained through the negotiations . . . that is to say, what you "must have" to be successful. Then, two other types of objectives can be established: functional or job-selected, and personal.

Long used by the Japanese culture in an attempt to create harmony and success, the elements of Hito (people), Kane (money), and Mano (things) are balanced in the optimal way to achieve goals. This tri-legged formula, as exhibited in Figure 4.4, can be applied to negotiation as a checkpoint for success.

The sharing of people, money, and things in an optimal way is the goal of any negotiation. It is each participant's *interest* in these elements which defines the boundaries of any negotiation. Take the simple example of money and a negotiation about how much some-one is willing to pay for a three bedroom home. This is particularly true if the potential buyer knows what the local financial institution is willing to lend. The range of potential options is depicted in Figure 4.5.

Regarding money then, the focus of the negotiations should be between $155,000 and $165,000. Perhaps the seller can accept a lower price if the buyer can close in three weeks (things) or is a relative (people). Maybe the buyer will pay a higher price if the seller can in fact hold a second mortgage on the property or is flexible on the closing date (things). Let's call this the *PMT Tradeoff*: it should be done every time you negotiate! Thus, the crux of negotiation lies in developing a game plan having both short- and long-term components, then testing and adjusting for circumstances and developments during the negotiation sessions.

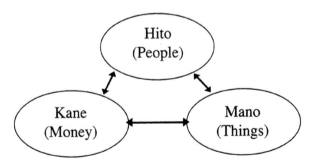

Figure 4.4

Balance the parties' interests in these elements and negotiating success is yours!

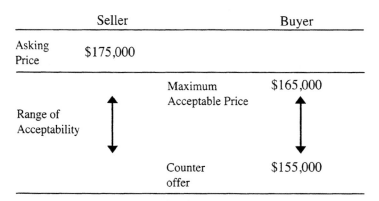

	Seller		Buyer
Asking Price	$175,000		
Range of Acceptability		Maximum Acceptable Price	$165,000
		Counter offer	$155,000
Minimal Acceptable Price	$150,000		

Figure 4.5

Range of Seller/Buyer Positions

Both of these types of objectives are subservient to the mandatory requirements and can be viewed as "would like to have" and "nice to have." They can be traded away to achieve higher level or more important objectives. As depicted in Figure 4.6, personal items can be traded for functional items which then can be traded to receive business critical items.

To elaborate on this point, assume that you were attempting to negotiate the lease of an office. What would your negotiating objectives be if your overall goal of the negotiation was to lease office space which was near prospective customers at a reasonable price?

Make up a list of objectives reflecting each of these concepts; that is, business, functional or job related, and personal. This is what our list would look like:

Business:	• Find space at reasonable rates (@ $18/SF)
	• Be close to customers (within 3-4 blocks)
Functional/Job Related:	• Provide as many corner offices as possible
	• Be on the first floor
	• Match leased space with company's style

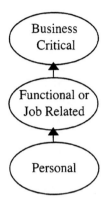

Figure 4.6

Negotiation Objective Setting Flow

Personal: • Locate the office in the most prestigious
                                     building with a river view
                                   • Finish the negotiations within two weeks

How did your list match up with ours? By reviewing both lists, it should be readily apparent that the lower level objectives can be logically traded away to ensure achievement of the business critical objectives.

4.5   IDENTIFYING AND INCLUDING STAKEHOLDERS

In order to set the proper goals and objectives, it will be necessary for you to identify the stakeholders, the individuals, or the functions within your company that will be affected by the negotiations in various ways, such as:

- Finance—Regarding payment terms and overall expenditure
- Engineering—Affecting specifications, design linkages, and technical support
- Manufacturing—Ensuring proper integration with company-made products and ability to make changes to out-sourced products
- Legal—Considering how best to protect the company's interests

- Marketing/Sales—Regarding the ability to meet ultimate customer's expectation
- Logistics—Ability to respond quickly to schedule changes and technical direction

If you are negotiating to buy a house, equipment, or any product or service for personal use, you are the primary stakeholder along with the members of your family or other interested parties. A stakeholder concern or expectation can be easily converted into a negotiation objective. Once established, these objectives can be managed, controlled, and maintained so that you can ensure that the results of the negotiations satisfy these individual or functional interests.

In fact, even if you cannot ensure that their individual desires will be met in the opening negotiations, you can at least inform them of the trade-offs made or being considered. Oftentimes, specific requirements of some stakeholders might need to be traded away to meet business objectives. This point was made earlier in our discussions on setting objectives.

Suppose you are attempting to purchase a piece of equipment to support your manufacturing plant and the manager of that function has specified that the selected equipment must be capable of being operated in a similar fashion as other equipment on the floor. The manager has been adamant about this requirement because of previous purchases which have resulted in equipment being installed without the operators being able to operate it. What might you do to invent alternate solutions during negotiations?

One possible solution could be hands-on training provided by the supplier after the equipment is installed. You could offer to accept this option once you have checked with the manufacturing manager and received approval. This could save your company money and result in higher efficiencies.

Suppose you are buying a house and each of your children has requested his or her own room. If you have a family of five people and are faced with choices among houses which have only three bedrooms (assume one bedroom for the parents and two other bedrooms for three children), you will definitely run into a problem with room allocation. Two of your children will lose out—unless you are creative and develop options with their interests in mind. There are quite a few options, all of which could be presented to the stakeholders (each of your children). Some possibilities include:

- Reassign the rooms every year so that someone new has a private room each year.
- Designate a part of the basement as a private area for one of the children who shares a room.
- Build another room at some point in the future.
- Allow one of the children to sleep outside (peferably, in a tent!) from time to time.
- Install a color TV or CD player in the shared bedroom.

You do have options. Being prepared, having these options available, and working with trade-offs will ensure satisfaction and mutually beneficial results for the people you represent.

4.6   STRATEGIC APPROACHES

A strategy describes how one is to accomplish his/her objectives. We are familiar with marketing or corporate strategy, or a person's strategy for an upcoming tennis match. . . . In these *areas,* a strategy consists of the actions we will take to ensure that the objective—i.e., to win the match, to launch a new product, or to become the best financial services firm in the United States—will be accomplished. The same holds true for negotiation strategy.

In Fisher and Ury's outstanding treatise on negotiations, *Getting to Yes,* they outlined a strategy to achieve objectives:

- Insist on accomplishing your interests, not achieving your pre-set position.
- Focus on the negotiation problem, not the people trying to solve the problem.
- Use objective criteria to evaluate different options and to set negotiable targets.

This work changed the way people in the field view and manage negotiation processes. We want to build on these components in our strategic approach.

Not everyone approaches negotiation in the same way. Some people use only one approach—the hard-driving, aggressive, don't give up anything, you lose/I win approach that still dominates the business landscape. The other approach is one of capitulation and over-cooperativeness which is often indicative of a lack of desire to negotiate.

The authors were asked by a leading Fortune 100 company to present a negotiation training program. Taking the lead from their corporate "award winning" policy on quality, they asked us to portray a win/win approach between buyer and seller in the upcoming negotiation training. They wanted to assist a subsidiary which made products for the automobile industry. In the course of our work with them, they lamented that the major needs of their customers during negotiations was to reduce cost. Their major clients, primarily Big Three automotive companies, took an aggressive win/lose approach. In any event, this company wanted to use the same aggressive approach with its suppliers. We applauded the client's representative for his noble effort to change the culture, but when we suggested that the participants use a participatory win/win, or *Getting To Yes* style, they completely rebelled, choosing to revert to the aggressive hard approach used by the customers. This is an example of how some companies reflect their customers' negotiation style, even though it might provide detrimental results.

We assert that although the hard, aggressive style may result in more favorable short–term benefit, it simply won't ensure a lasting, beneficial, growing relationship with others. Just think back about when you have conducted negotiations in the win/lose manner. How sustainable were the results in the long term?

Accordingly, we believe that you should be prepared to:
1. Meet the hard-charging aggressive approach head on.
2. Effectively deal with the overly cooperative approach so the other party gains something positive from the negotiation.
3. Accept the fact that in some cases, you will not be able to change the course much when dealing with individuals possessing the hard-charging approaches. Focus them on the ensuing negotiation opportunity.

Negotiation is an interpersonal skill . . . it is the practice of discussions between two or more human beings who bring to the table their own particular experiences, preferences, priorities, and cultures. A "cookie cutter" or standardized approach to strategy-setting will not work in this situation. This is not to say that we should not prepare for a negotiation in a way that will achieve a sustainable win/win result for both parties. We must, however, recognize that until and unless individuals realize the benefits of developing synergistic results by establishing long-term focused relationships and trustful communications, the chances of realistically achieving win/win outcomes are minimal.

So what then, should you do to set your strategy? Should your prepare for the *worst* or the *best* situation? The correct answer is *neither.* Much of the popular writing on negotiations has recommended various styles like autocratic, bureaucratic, gamesman, etc. and tactics like good guy-bad guy, segment the problem, surprise, walk out, and so on. We choose not to adopt these pop-psych prescriptions, but will focus on describing the elements of an effective strategy instead.

In order to develop a negotiation strategy, the following questions apply:

1. In *what* manner will you treat the other party?
2. *How* are you going to influence the other party to consider your key points?
3. *When* will you discuss the salient interests and objectives of the parties?
4. *Where* will you accomplish the negotiation sessions?
5. *Why* should the parties reach a final agreement?

Following this simple what, when, why, where, and how model will provide an effective implementable strategy for you and/or your team.

The way you treat someone in negotiations is an ethical decision. It goes straight to the notion of fairness, reasonableness, equity, and how you as an individual want to be treated. It would be simple to take the view that you need to be competitive or extremely aggressive, and that you need to get the most for your company or for your team to the detriment of the other party. But this has been proven to be short-lived in its effect. Over the long term, you will not be effective, the other party will want to negotiate with someone else, your style will be viewed as uncompromising and obnoxious, or you simply will not be effective because you will not have the upper hand in terms of time, information, or power. Today's relationships are long term and are frequently the subject of intense negotiation. Today's negotiations will have dramatic effects, but over time circumstances will change. The negotiation procedings will remain in the record so *how you treat others* will matter in terms of *how you will be treated* and *viewed* over the long term.

Being fair and reasonable does not mean that you can't be tough on the problem or situation at hand. It means directing your aggressive efforts to solving a problem. Effective teamwork can be ensured by carefully managing the negotiation process. While aggressively seeking solutions you must consider the effects your efforts have on the other party.

Suppose you are a member of a team of people within your company attempting to negotiate resources and you press hard, use all possible tactics, and are uncompromising. You may get the resources, but you will be a short-term hero for your function, at the expense of others. What will happen the next time resources are divided? You will be ganged up on, bludgeoned, decimated—in other words, the other parties will be *ready* for you, bonding together to give you the short end of the stick. It is likely that these effects will continue to prevail until you change your approach.

4.7 PLANNING FOR NEGOTIATING WITHIN TEAMS

In today's business world, teaming abounds. It is a common thread seen throughout large and small companies, governments, suppliers, and non-profit organizations. Even sports organizations are using team relationships with their individual members to develop structured roles and negotiations.

We believe that to be an effective team member, you must master the art of negotiations. If you are to properly participate, you must first define your role in the team. If you are a team leader, you must determine the capabilities of the entire team, determine what is to be done, and then define the roles and responsibilities of team members. Typical questions in the case where your team is negotiating on behalf of an organization include the following:

1. What educational background and business experience is necessary?
2. Who will assume the lead negotiator role?
3. Who will provide support, and in what form?
4. What planning steps must be done?
5. Who among the team members has a personal stake in the results?

We think that team members must be committed to the completion of the negotiations, and possess something of value which is dealt with in the negotiation itself. Without this "stake" in the results, the quality of the negotiation outcome will suffer and perhaps not be implemented. You might also lose control of the whole process. The expectations of negotiations among members of a cross-functional team, say, to develop a new service process or to build a shipping center take on different characteristics. In this case the task is to attain a win/win settlement within the team rather than with an outside party. The questions also appear differently:

1. What are the mutual needs of the team members? What are the individual unique needs?
2. Who has what at stake?
3. What techniques might be useful to complete a satisfactory outcome?
   - Brainstorming
   - Group Consensus
   - Conference
4. What quality tools can be utilized?
5. Are there any team decisions or procedures that have to be made/set which could influence the outcome?

We have briefly dealt with the aspects of negotiation planning associated with teams whether they were involved in negotiating as a team or agreeing on a distribution of value for team members. By considering the needs of the team members, and using the entire negotiating process we have outlined, team success will be almost guaranteed.

Getting Ready—Organizing for Effective Negotiation

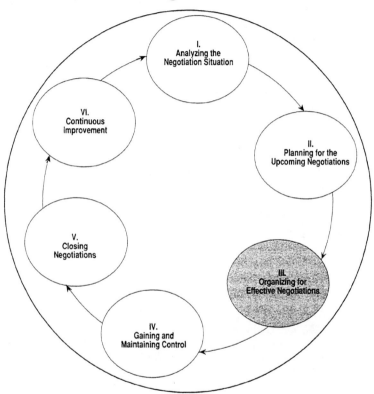

5.1 STAFFING THE NEGOTIATION TEAM

It is a truism that a plan is only as good as the people who must carry it out. One of the critical factors in ensuring negotiation success is the assignment of the responsibility to the person(s) most likely to succeed.

Who will be on your team? Once again we must distinguish between small-scale or personal negotiations and large-scale team negotiations in which your cause will be represented by a number of role players. In the latter case, you should include those qualified individuals needed to provide the functional expertise to deal with any problems that are likely to surface during the negotiations. Such expertise may also be needed to present the case you are preparing to make in the best light. Typically, in a business situation, the sales, purchasing, or other personnel carrying the negotiation burden must be supported by legal, financial, and technical experts (e.g., engineering, manufacturing, or quality control) as the particular case requires. Although it may appear plausible to "wing it" alone, it is more prudent to err on the side of overkill as far as supporting expertise is concerned. This is particularly true when dealing with matters crucial to either the negotiator's personal concern or the company's future well being, or even survival.

In the team approach it is important to assign an individual to lead the planning effort. The leadership role includes calling meetings, establishing and maintaining a planning schedule, assigning responsibility for research and preparation, developing agendas for meetings, and making final decisions regarding issue positions and the structure of the negotiation framework. The leader may or may not be designated as the chief negotiator but in our experience these roles are usually assigned to the same person.

It must be recognized however, that, frequently, the individual who is the most effective planner, or has superior management skills, is not always blessed with the verbal acuity and histrionic talents required of a spokesperson. In these cases, it would be wise to appoint a skilled negotiator to handle the presentations under the watchful eye of the negotiations manager described above. It is important, moreover, that team activities and communications be strictly controlled during a multifaceted complex negotiation. This concept must be firmly entrenched during the planning phase during which the timing of offers, counter offers, and issue repackaging is carefully orchestrated. Thus, each participant must be fully aware of his/her role in carrying out the game plan.

In contrast to these large team efforts, some negotiations are frequently planned and executed by one person, which is often the case in small companies or in matters involving relatively little money. In such situations of course, organization is not an issue. But the solo negotiator, in getting ready for an important negotiation session, will be wise to consider all of the principles of organization described here, since he/she will confront many of the problems faced by a negotiating team. The task will be much more difficult for the solo negotiator since the needed technical support and assistance in reading signals and/or restructuring strategy will not be available. On the other hand, the lone negotiator has the advantage of not having to worry about controlling team members who may cause distractions or serve as targets of diversionary tactics by the opposition. Some negotiators feel comfortable only in the solo role. They should not, however, shortchange the role of support in the planning stage.

5.2 DEVELOPING A GAME PLAN

Once the negotiation team is established, (including the solo negotiator situation) the primary task is to develop a game plan. This is the part of the process that places the various issues in the negotiation framework as a function of their relative importance, and creates a logic for concessions, offers, counter offers, and ultimate agreement. The game plan includes an agenda, which implicitly schedules the timing of subjects for discussion, thus creating a scenario for the most favorable presentation of the planner's case.

Uppermost in the planner's mind are the basic goals to be achieved in the upcoming session. As described in the planning process, the goals are expressed in terms of specific objectives. The game plan is devised to optimize the chances of attaining these objectives, while remaining fully aware of the position of the other party.

To examine a simple game plan let us create a framework similar to what is indicated in Figure 5.1 for the major league baseball negotiation we discussed earlier. We will examine the case from the owner's perspective.

Owners' Objectives	Players' Objectives
• Salary ceiling for each club	• Attainment of free agency in shorter time
• Revenue sharing—Large-market teams share TV revenue with small-market teams	• Earlier eligibility for arbitration
	• Increase owners' contribution to retirement fund
• Contributions to charities in players' names	• Higher minimum salary levels
• Individual performance incentives for payment	• Compensation during non-league games
• Players' community service without compensation	• Meal allowances, work rules liberalized

Figure 5.1

Owners' and Players' Negotiation Objectives

  The game plan for the owners would be designed to enhance the chances for adoption of its primary objective—the salary cap. What is the best way to present this issue? If presented as the opening move, it could turn off the players' representatives who, concluding that little agreement was possible, would harden their position and call for a strike. There could be arguments, therefore, in the agenda planning session for presenting the revenue-sharing later in the session. If some minor item on the agenda was first sold to the players, conceivably the atmosphere could be more cordial, and some agreements reached. In such an atmosphere even the salary cap could finally be accepted, perhaps with some modification.

Based on some presumed strategic thinking, the elements to be included in the game plan would be as follows:

Agenda

- Statement of opposing position by each side.
- Placement of issues on the table for discussion, and in what order.
- Solicitation of reaction from other side.
- Discussion of issues important to the other side.
- Our reaction to their proposals.
- Break for initial discussion of opponents' position and perhaps restructuring of own position.
- Return to table with new package:
  - Attempt to sell salary cap by accepting other issues important to players.
- If no agreement reached, suggest a break in which players are invited to submit new proposal. Encourage them to package it to their own liking, thus allowing them to make acceptance without abject surrender.
- Return to table and attempt to close, based on opposition's counter proposal.
- Continue to conclusion.

The game plan would also include the identity of a spokesperson for each phase and the timing of away-from-the-table events, such as press conferences, releases to the press, etc. As in most high-profile disputes, a great deal of the negotiation is done outside the meeting room, in attempts to capture the support of the interested public and thus create pressure (on opponents) for acceptance.

The game plan described here would be part of the Negotiation Plan similar to the sample outlined in Figure 5.2. This document provides a framework for identifying the key players, issues, and logistics details. The game plan would be a key part of this document.

Subject Matter: _____

Target Date for Negotiation: _____

1.0 Requirement

Product/Service: _____

Description: _____

Quantity: _____

Delivery: _____

2.0 Negotiation Objectives (What are you trying to negotiate?)

A. _____

B. _____

C. _____

D. _____

E. _____

3.0 Stakeholders to Negotiation

Stakeholders	**Stakeholder Requirements**
A. _____	A. _____
B. _____	B. _____
C. _____	C. _____
D. _____	D. _____

4.0 Negotiation Team Members

Name	**Function**
_____	_____
_____	_____
_____	_____
_____	_____
_____	_____

Figure 5.2

Negotiation Plan

5.0 Price Negotiation Objectives

Buyer Initial Position: _____

Buyer Fallback Position: _____

Buyer Walkaway Position: _____

6.0 Items to be Negotiated

	Targets	**Initial**
Purchase Price:	_____	_____
Lead-Time Commitment:	_____	_____
Quality Performance Goal:	_____	_____
Reliability Performance Goal:	_____	_____
Service:	_____	_____
On-Time Delivery Goal:	_____	_____
Lead-Time Reduction Goal:	_____	_____
Value Analysis/Cost-Reduction Goal:	_____	_____
Inventory Reduction Initiatives:	_____	_____
Other:	_____	_____
	_____	_____
	_____	_____

7.0 Tactics to be Used

Outset of/During Negotiations: _____

_____

_____

_____

Conclusion of Negotiations: _____

_____

_____

_____

Figure 5.2

Negotiation Plan

Continued

This plan is typical of what is required in a high-stakes negotiation in which each side has a great deal to win or lose. The elements described here—listing of objectives, timing for their discussion, fall-back procedures, and logic for reaching conclusion which is acceptable to both sides—should be used in any negotiations, but especially those in which a number of issues must be considered and settled. The planner must come up with a detailed plan that will give his/her position the best chance of prevailing. At the same time he/she must consider those aspects of the opponent's position that can be accepted, thus achieving a win/win result.

In the tragic Branch Davidian Waco incident, there is little evidence that anyone ever considered a more reasonable outcome was possible.

When the Bureau of Alcohol, Tobacco, and Firearms entered into their eleventh day of negotiations with cult leader David Koresh, they were faced with an ever-changing situation. At that point in time, they were still wondering what Koresh wanted and also whether what they could ultimately provide to him was a more attractive offer than a martyr's death.

Most news agencies really blasted the U.S. Government negotiators, but a key element was missing here . . . . meaningful communication. Questions surfaced as to whether Koresh was "readable" or whether he was interested in surviving at all. We believe that the mistake made by the negotiators was negotiating with Koresh at all . . . the other individuals in the compound were the ones to talk to. They had things—people, children, lives—at stake. So perhaps the plan had to be redrawn to consider this possibility. A different strategy of enlarging the communication and feedback channels may also have helped. The government controlled most of the negotiations through a small band of authorized negotiators gathered in temporary trailers.

The strategy normally applied is to use a team of negotiators who rely on outside experts, rather than bringing in outsiders to help negotiate directly. This in the end might be what caused the ultimate failure of the negotiations from the government's perspective. The government negotiators were just too close, having lost three of their compatriots, and continuous name-calling and broken promises prevailed. An outsider could have provided a fresh, independent perspective. We know that this view may contradict a previous point or the need for the negotiators to have something at stake. No laws are truly universal in negotiations so we would make an exception here. It would have been wise to draw up a new, fresh plan targeted at the Koresh supporters.

Some of the items to consider here should have been:

1. Koresh members knew that they would face life imprisonment if they surrendered, due to the killing of federal agents.
2. Followers of Koresh had been extraordinarily logical.
3. Koresh and his followers were living in familiar surroundings and were comfortable.
4. The ultimate settlement had to be satisfactory from a biblical or religious point of view.

As the *New York Times* reporter, Peter Applebome, reported, negotiators are "eternal optimists." He predicted that negotiators will have the view that there will always be another tactic and always another brainstorm which can be developed to assist in negotiations. But as history will record it, time ran out on the negotiation plans with Koresh. Using a tank to begin to demolish the buildings, ultimately led up to the destruction of the Koresh enclave by the members of the sect themselves.

5.3 ENSURING THE COMPLETENESS AND CURRENCY OF THE PLAN

In structuring the plan it is important to acquire all information which will affect the negotiations. Such information would include any business plans that the opposition has made public or any rumors that have emerged. It would also include personal information, such as, in the sale of a home, the seller's plans to relocate or change marital status. The point here is not to encourage unsavory or illegal investigations, but to be aware of public information which could affect the opposition's motivation. Such knowledge would be of great value to a negotiator in assessing what is attainable in a negotiation and what position the opposition is likely to take.

We are aware of an historic example of the crucial effect of missing one piece of information in an otherwise superb plan. On June 4, 1942, a huge Japanese fleet sped towards Midway Island in the Pacific, headed for a showdown with the American Pacific Fleet. The upcoming engagement was subject to the most intensive planning imaginable. The U.S. Navy, having broken the Japanese code, was well aware of the enemy's intentions and battle plans: to invade Midway Island. The Japanese, having been successful less than six months earlier at Pearl Harbor, were confident that their planning was perfect. However, one key bit of information was missing from their plan: would American aircraft carriers be available to oppose the Japanese fleet and threaten the invasion?

Before dawn on the morning of the fourth, the Japanese decided to cancel a last-minute reconnaissance flight designed to determine the U.S. carriers' presence or absence. They thus gambled that the carriers were otherwise engaged and would not pose a problem.

Less than three hours later their gamble proved wrong. When they launched their attack on Midway they were stunned to be confronted by U.S. carrier planes. More importantly, they had neglected to arm their own planes with torpedoes and armor-piercing bombs for attacking ships. As a result, the Japanese lost four aircraft carriers in less than an half hour, changing the balance of Naval power in the Pacific and effectively determining the ultimate result of the war.

This is a classic example of flawed planning from the absence of key information. The negotiator must do the utmost to uncover every bit of information that will contribute to a successful plan. The negotiator must avoid surprise at all costs. That being said, since it is impossible to have perfect information, the plan must be flexible enough to accommodate new information as it arises, as well as unexpected moves by the opposition.

What do you do, as a negotiator, if in your planning, some important question arises to which you don't know the answer? We would suggest that you do all you can to obtain the answer, and if you don't get it, delay proceeding until all the information is in. In the battle of Midway, the Japanese commanders wished they had waited a few more hours, instead of proceeding to disaster.

Testing the Validity of the Plan

Planning is primarily a one-sided process—utilizing inputs from members of one side's team or stakeholders who would benefit from the team's success. The team may also solicit inputs from objective third parties who could provide some guidance as to the plan's prospects for success. Such observers could also detect errors in the approach which would not be readily evident to the plan's creators. The resulting plan is, hopefully, the best available in the eyes of its creators, sponsors, and neutral observers.

The acid test for the plan is its effectiveness in dealing with the opposition. It is, therefore, most important to obtain some sense of the other side's reactions to the idea presented, which will surely occur once the negotiations begin. At that point the plan's authors may learn that their thinking needs overhauling, in which case an altered plan must emerge.

While this is valuable learning procedure, it would be preferable to have some idea of the opposition's probable response during the planning stage so that objectives can be stated at realistic levels with some possibility of attainment. However, it is no simple matter to determine the thinking of the opposition prior to actual negotiations. Let us consider, then, some techniques that may be used to learn what the reaction is likely to be. How it is done varies with the type of negotiations being planned.

Testing the Plan: Two-Person Limited Focus Negotiation

In a personal, one-dimensional negotiation, a phone call can be used to test the waters. The object would be to determine the disposition of the other party. Does he/she sound receptive? Is he/she going to be tough, friendly, or non-committal? Some good questions would be:

- "What are you going to be looking for in this negotiation?"
- "Is there anything you need from us to get ready?"
- "Let me tell you how I see this going, and maybe you could let me know if we seem to be going in opposite directions."

It would be useful to keep the conversation on a friendly, professional level to set the stage for progress in the upcoming meeting. Out of such contact can come a better sense of the probable response to the plan and provide the groundwork for making alterations as necessary. If, for example, the other party is going to have serious objections, it is important to know this, so that it can be accommodated in your planning.

If the other party is someone the planner has never dealt with, it would be useful to consult with colleagues or co-workers who have dealt with that individual or firm in the past. Other sources of information would include:

- Records of past dealings with that company
- Dun and Bradstreet reports
- Press reports on the other party indicating their earnings and sales records; and concerning new products, expansion plans, capacity utilization rates, business setbacks, etc.
- Various information sources providing automated data on companies

Much of this discussion deals with negotiations representing companies or institutions. The principles and methods outlined here can also be utilized in personal negotiations. The basic point is that contact and research prior to an actual negotiation can be quite valuable in planning a negotiation and the other party's likely response to it. At all costs, you should avoid surprises. It is an old saying among trial lawyers that you should never ask a question to which you don't know the answer. Negotiators should heed the same advice.

Testing the Plan: Large-Scale Team Negotiations

Determining the opposition's probable stance during the planning stage is even more important in large-scale, high-profile negotiations because planning is so costly and time-consuming that pains must be taken to optimize the investment in getting ready. In such situations a *preliminary meeting* is useful. Here, both sides send a representative to discuss the upcoming session and to lay out ground rules regarding time, place, duration of meeting, tentative agenda, personnel attending, and logistics. The meeting will not only ease the transition into serious negotiations but will also provide an opportunity for probing the likely attitude of the opposition. In the final negotiations between the U.S. and North Vietnam, six months were devoted to determining the shape of the table in the upcoming session. Critics have suggested the issue was a ruse to stall for changes in the military situation before the serious negotiations began. At any rate, the Vietnamese attitude toward the table shape was a strong signal of their feelings toward more serious issues. In addition to preliminary meetings, phone calls are a useful pre-meeting device in large-scale negotiations.

In negotiations receiving much public attention, such as mergers and takeovers, conflicts between governments, and strikes and lockouts, special tactics are employed to test the opposition's attitude. These tactics include leaks to the press, formal news releases, press conferences, trial balloons, and legal maneuvers such as filing for injunctions or law suits. These devices are often used to ferret out the other party's position as part of the planning process. It should be noted, however, that these activities, though often occurring prior to the actual start of negotiations, are really part of the negotiation itself. In short, much of the negotiating in these disputes that capture the public's imagination is done in the press, on television, in the halls of Congress, etc. These media provide a useful forum for testing negotiation strategies prior to making them part of a formal plan or trying out new approaches after the negotiations have begun.

A trial run is another device for assessing probable opposition attitudes. This technique involves conducting a mock negotiation with a team made up of either colleagues or consultants retained to represent the opposition and respond to the presentation of the in-house team. This feedback is vital to assessing the reasonableness of the planned offer(s) and the effectiveness of the proposed strategy.

The use of such testing is quite common in industry. Companies facing important legal disputes regarding patent ownership or contractual interpretations frequently stage mock trials with lawyers for both sides, juries made up of hired individuals with the appropriate demographic profile and law professors in the role of judges. These mock trials are useful in developing strategies for upcoming cases, or determining whether a particular legal course should be continued or abandoned. An important negotiation, crucial to a company's future, should receive similar attention.

Another precedent for trial runs is the use of "red teams" in the preparation of high-dollar proposals to potential customers. In this technique, widely used among large defense contractors, an in-house team is created to play the role of customer officials representing technical, financial, and legal interests to respond to the proposal and suggest changes, where needed. Any company facing an important, complex negotiation with a customer or supplier would find the red team approach useful. It would be particularly valuable to negotiations planners since the red team could react not only to the content of the negotiation framework, but also to the timing and presentation of issues. The red team should include experienced negotiators, particularly some who have dealt with the customer or supplier involved.

All of these testing techniques are valuable in shaping the game plan and providing some insight into how the other party is likely to react. Although we have concentrated on the high stakes formal negotiations in discussing these techniques, we would point out that some testing is useful in planning the simplest one-on-one negotiation. In addition to the warm-up phone call we mentioned, there is also a letter confirming an appointment in which some preliminary information could be launched for some possible reaction. Finally, there is the opportunity for trying your approach on a colleague who could role play as the other side. Even the simplest but highly personal negotiations, such as car shopping, renting an apartment, or interviewing for a job, deserve some careful planning and testing before one enters the negotiation arena.

5.4   ADJUSTING THE PLAN

A plan is most useful when it is a flexible dynamic document, responsive to situational changes as they occur. Such flexibility must be built into the plan as a result of preliminary assessments of the opposition's probable response. Thus, the plan will go through several modifications before reaching its final format. It is important that in drafting the negotiations plan, the planner incorporate all new intelligence uncovered by pre-negotiations probing, peer reviews, and reactions by mentors and colleagues familiar with the other party or experienced in negotiating with them. The final plan will thus be as current as possible and will contain fall-back positions based on expected concessions that the negotiator can live with and support with logical analysis. The negotiator must also be prepare to revise his/her plan during the course of the negotiations when circumstances beyond the control of the negotiators present themselves.

When the previously discussed Bell-Atlantic–TCI negotiations took place, two basic parts of the deal were significant:
- How much TCI was worth
- How much Bell-Atlantic was willing to pay

The negotiators representing both parties were not prepared at these negotiations to adjust their plans. Bell Atlantic proposed to issue some 200 million new class B shares, but the stock lost ground before the new shares were issued. It fell 20% of its value. TCI was asking for the release of more shares to make up the difference. Bell-Atlantic proposed that TCI was worth less than previously thought. Both parties were reacting to an unforeseen event, at least up this point, in new government rules affecting the rates charged by cable companies. Were these negotiators armed with more flexible plans, the negotiations would have included more innovative options.

5.5   BE READY FOR SURPRISES

One fascinating aspect of negotiations is that surprises are a part of the game. This fact underscores the need for flexibility and the ability to adjust to new situations. Let us illustrate with a rather surprising example. A client of ours in a Defense Department weapons command had solicited proposals for a moderately sized study (budgeted for about $3 million) from a number of firms. One firm's technical proposal was clearly superior to the others. While its price was higher, it was determined that they should be awarded the contract. Accordingly, the firm was invited in for discussions, in which the government hoped to reduce the price. This incident occurred in the 1970s during a period of high inflation in the U.S.

Upon arrival at the negotiation meeting, the prospective contractor had a surprise for his customer. After friendly introductions around the bargaining table, the contractor representative announced he was submitting (and placed on the table) a revised proposal with a price that was almost 10% higher than his original submission. He explained to his stunned hosts that his management felt the adjustment was necessary in view of rapidly rising costs during the lengthy period of solicitation and proposal preparation.

A spirited discussion followed in which the government insisted they would only consider the original submission and would not entertain an increased price offer. The contractor argued as forcibly that his response was justified. The discussion continued for some time in which the ethics of one party and unreasonableness of the other were alternately challenged. Eventually, a truce was called for separate deliberations, after which the government announced they would only discuss the original proposal. After some final pleading, the contractor representative agreed ruefully that they would fall back to their original position. The group then took up the discussion of the original proposal and after a relatively brief period of questions and answers the government accepted the proposal with minor revisions.

It is interesting to review what happened here. Was the revised proposal submission a trick to upset the opposition? What happened to the government's plan? Were they ready for the unexpected? What about the contractor's plan? Did it include a request for upward revision which would then be bargained downward, but not all the way back to the original?

If we examine the result, we must conclude that the contractor's plan was successful. By submitting an outrageous last minute price increase, he upset the opposition, and directed discussion towards his new unacceptable offer. After some heated discussions the government was only too happy to consider the original proposal which now appeared much more attractive than at first view.

This case illustrates the need for flexibility in planning. "What if" questions should be raised and fall-back positions prepared, for coping with moves that the opposition could make. The plan should at least allow for tactical surprises from the opposition and some thought be given to how they should be handled. As a final post-script to this example we should note the lasting effect a tactic such as this would have on relations between parties. This experience would obviously be a factor in assessing the environmental factors surrounding future negotiations.

Getting it Done:
Gaining and Maintaining Control

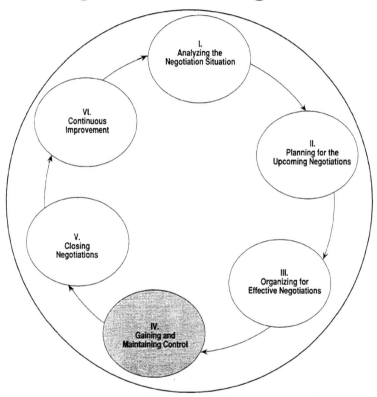

Have you ever been involved in a negotiation where subjects are brought up, discussed, and dropped without any regard to time, priorities, and relevance to the main issues at hand? Have you ever seen people speaking out of turn with no clear idea of who's in charge? If you have, you were experiencing a negotiation out of control.

Control is an interesting word when it pertains to negotiations. We use the word to describe how to drive a car, the way to ensure financial integrity of a company, and as method of ensuring that your football team has possession of the ball over 50% of the allotted game time. When we "control," we usually follow a pre-ordained strategy. We employ tactics. We influence others to believe as we do. Finally, we usually can measure whether or not we are in control by tabulating how many minutes we are in possession of the football, the smoothness and safety of the car trip, and the extent to which we experienced unauthorized expenditures within a company.

Control, in negotiations, means to influence the flow, timing, and content of the negotiations process. To control requires careful planning and a bona fide strategy. Control, then, just does not happen by itself. There absolutely has to be more structure or basis for it. In negotiations, you must first gain control of the process, then you must maintain it (*don't lose it*) over the course of negotiations.

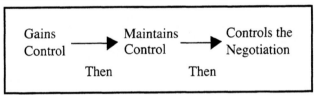

Figure 6.1

The Significance of Control

Figure 6.1 does not suggest that by control we mean the process of "winning" the negotiation. Rather, the term implies orchestrating the process so the result is a good one and preferably providing satisfaction to both parties.

6.1 GAINING CONTROL

To gain control, as we have suggested earlier, requires a carefully crafted idea of what you need to accomplish in negotiations and how you might go about achieving these goals during the course of negotiations. The best place to start is at the beginning of the negotiation process, when you know you are going to negotiate with someone/some organization. We addressed the interworkings of strategy development in Chapter 4. In this chapter we stress that you have to *implement* the strategy, *roll it out,* and *employ* it in the negotiations.

To a great extent, by working with the other party to define the interests and expected outcomes, you can dramatically "control" the early stages of the negotiating process. Some of the work here includes:

1. Scheduling strategy or goal setting meetings
2. Providing drafts of points of interest and interest statements
3. Reviewing strategy with internal customers
4. Gaining consensus on the criteria against which the final negotiated outcome can be judged

If both parties participate equally in these activities, they greatly improve the likelihood that they will achieve the intended results and ensure that the negotiation process contains all the necessary features. They make this possible by including reasonable agendas and procedures to deliver the desirable outcomes. The existence of a strategy or plan, in this context, works like a vision or target for the parties. Without a strategy or plan, there typically are not the logical steps in place to give the parties enough confidence that they are making appropriate progress toward their goals. To reach this confidence or comfort level, they must constantly suggest, agree, debate, and reject ideas. They must do this to improve the critical elements of negotiation including:

- Agenda Items
- Timing
- Location
- Participants
- Roles and Responsibilities
- Level of Management Involvement
- Measurements of Progress
- Data Requirements
- Tactics
- Stakeholder Requirements
- Goals, Objectives

- Formula Used For Calculation
- Follow-up Action Items

This is an extensive list of discussion points to be dealt with once negotiations begin. We are not saying that you can *eliminate* all of them, but you can reduce the number of these items, by properly planning in the front end of the process.

While we are stressing techniques for gaining control at the outset of negotiations, we must emphasize the importance of never losing sight of your original goal(s). Your goals are the reason the strategy was developed in the first place. If the strategy is not working, consider first how the strategy can be changed or slightly altered to be effective. If any set of changes cannot be effective, then review the goals. Perhaps they are unrealistic, outdated, or impossible, given the circumstances. It might be time to reframe the goals, after discussing the status with your key internal customers and stakeholders. From a flow chart standpoint, it might look like what is indicated in Figure 6.2.

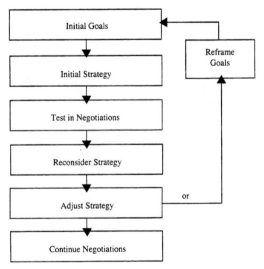

Figure 6.2

How to Gain Control.

During the course of negotiations, goals and strategies can change remarkably. This all depends on the complexity of the negotiations, history, precedent, political sensitivity, and institutionalization, or experience level of the negotiators. These types of changes have occurred in the following well-known negotiations:

Situation	Goals		Strategic Approach	
• United States Treasury Agents vs. David Koresh (1994)	From:	Convince to Surrender	From:	Wait them out, negotiate through emissaries
	To:	Containment	To:	Demand surrender, contain with overwhelming force
• U.S.–Japan Trade (1993-94)	• Improved balance of trade (from U.S. perspective) by opening Japanese markets (no change)		From:	Specific guidelines on quotas
			To:	General frameworks for discussion
• Health Care Coverage for all Americans (President vs. Congress 1994)	From:	Universal coverage at all costs	From:	High-powered task force developing detailed plan
	To:	Quality of care for all citizens at affordable costs	To:	Maneuvering with Congress for pieces of plan with view to special interests

At the time of this writing, the David Koresh negotiations had completely failed. The government had abandoned its containment goal and adopted an aggressive strategy to disarm and seek a surrender from the people in the Waco compound. In studying the course of negotiations we observed that both the goals and strategies were changing without a formal evaluation of the impact of these changes on either party.

The outcome might have been different had the U.S. Treasury agents attained some control of the negotiation team through rational discussion of the issues to be resolved. No reasonable negotiations were ever conducted and perhaps were not possible given the personalities involved and the violent nature of the initial confrontation. The case is interesting, however, since it showed the devastating effect of the absence of a controlling agenda and some mutuality of interest in achieving a nonviolent outcome. In other words, control was never achieved by either party. It was somewhat similar to the Iranian hostage situation because of the degree of religious fanaticism involved.

The health care coverage issue suffered not only from a shift in strategy but also from a failure to negotiate sincerely. When the issue was finally joined in late 1994 and Congress responded to the plan, too much negotiating had gone on in the media through advertising campaigns, press releases, and public forums. During the months the task force was developing the plan (effectively, in secret) opponents of a health care plan could attack it with impunity. When the plan was finally revealed, so much animosity had been created and so much momentum gained by the opposition, that the plan was doomed to failure.

This was a classic example of non-negotiating. Our position has been that planning, although done in a vacuum, must be tested on the opposition before it is finalized. If the opposition is allowed to contribute to its development they feel some responsibility for it and think somewhat better of it. The health care experience also illustrates the importance of environmental factors in assessing the acceptability of one's position. As subsequent events confirmed, 1994 was not a year in which effective negotiation between political parties was feasible. The case also suggests there was a loss of focus on the part of the health plan developers who were hung up on details. This added to the detriment of the major strategic goal—health care coverage for all Americans.

The Role of Agendas in Maintaining Control

In addition to the pre–negotiation activities to establish control, the negotiator must utilize the tools at his or her disposal to keep and maintain control of the discussions once they have begun. One of the most valuable tools for ensuring controls is the negotiation *agenda*. It is, however only one of a number of control influencing items that should have been established. An inclusive list follows.

- A prepared agenda, circulated in advance
- Clearly stated objectives (from strategy setting)
- Clearly defined time limits (from strategy setting)
- Clearly understood roles (from strategy setting)
- Flip charts, overheads, white boards, and other visual aids
- Some means of keeping a permanent record (e.g., minutes)
- A seating arrangement conducive to the group process

Setting the agenda is the most significant part of preparing for an upcoming negotiation session. The purpose of the agenda is to focus the negotiation session; in its absence, the result is a fuzzy, disjointed session. Agendas limit discussion to the most important issues being addressed. They control the flow of the discussion by delineating the order and timing of each item and they set the course of discussion.

> Rule: There should be an agenda established
>   for every negotiation meeting, session,
>   and discussion.

6.2   You Set the Agenda With Their Help

You should ask the party if they would be agreeable to your preparing the agenda. Let them react to that question. They will probably agree to your proposition but request subsequent review and approval of it prior to distribution. Agendas can vary from informal to formal, simple to complex (with attachments) and short or long. You can make that judgment based upon what is to be negotiated. We believe that it is an excellent idea to have both parties agree with the agenda before it is published or introduced.

We can summarize these points as follows:

1. An agenda is a step-by-step outline of how you wish to proceed.
2. It is a personal guide to achieve your goals.
3. The agenda should reflect the interests of the other party.
4. An agenda is a control mechanism to help ensure that the negotiation proceeds in earnest and at a sufficient pace.

The format for an agenda, as we have mentioned, depends on the nature of what is being negotiated. Generally speaking, however, the format would include the following information.

1. Date
2. Attendees of meeting
3. Time/location of session
4. Short description of subject/topics
5. Order of discussion of subjects
6. Length of time for each topic
7. Start and end time

Agendas are typically presented in memorandum form. Do allow for enough "white" space in the memo itself so that the words "jump out" at the reader.

Exercise:

Prepare an agenda for an upcoming negotiation session, either one which is in process or one which is just beginning.

Have another person review your draft . . . confirm that they understand the purpose of the meeting and can make some reasonable assumptions about expected results from the meeting.

Make sure that you confirm the agenda with the other party; list every attendee's name (you don't want to offend anyone), confirm attendance, date, time, and meeting location. Open the negotiation session with another brief review and ratification of the agenda. Once underway, monitor the time allotted for each topic. Don't allow discussion to digress, unless all parties agree to do so or decide to reschedule the discussion for a later session. Once points are disputed, record the other party's views; you can then restate for understanding. Don't analyze or editorialize until the appropriate time. Try to stick to the agenda and redirect discussion when necessary. If you are leading the session, guide the discussion being careful not to "over-control" things.

In order to begin to identify areas for agreement, consider Figure 6.3, which describes a useful set of stages to ensure some sense of control in negotiation sessions.

The agenda is a key success factor in effective meeting management. In any meeting or, in our parlance, negotiation session, you should endeavor to create an open and candid atmosphere, where individuals are cordial and cooperative with each other. If possible, these notions can be integrated into the *rules* which the parties agree to at the outset of negotiations. We believe that attention to "creature" comforts, low formality, and a stated preference for interpersonal relationship building will usher these notions along.

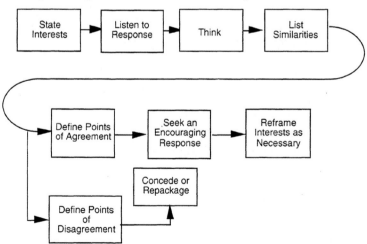

Figure 6.3

Flow of Negotiations Meeting Session

Be sure to look out for stress and stress-infected agenda items, a high degree of structure and formality, any attempt to kill interaction, pressure being applied by either party inappropriately, or others yielding to stronger personalities. In short, be attentive to any activity/behavior/development which could disturb the control you are seeking.

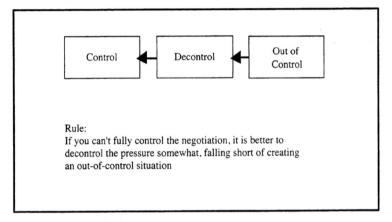

Rule:
If you can't fully control the negotiation, it is better to decontrol the pressure somewhat, falling short of creating an out-of-control situation

6.3 REGAINING CONTROL—AN EXAMPLE

After eighteen months of a contractual relationship with a supplier to Motorola, the supplier announced that the previously established discount would be reduced by 5% due to reduced business volume. In the meeting that followed this announcement, the Motorola purchasing manager developed three questions for discussions:

1. Was the product a stable product, standardized with little change requested?
2. Was the product a mature product so that new products are being introduced as replacement products?
3. Had the product shown continuous improvement?

The manager asked these questions in the initial negotiations, received positive answers to each, and thus gained control of the negotiations. He responded that based on the "Yes" responses, the cost of quality had continually been reduced, thereby lowering the cost of ownership, and therefore expected that the discounts be maintained. He was able to resolve the problem by getting the supplier to agree to hold his price. His tactic of using the agenda forced both parties to openly discuss costs and their mutual needs. This ultimately resulted in both parties achieving a win/win result.

6.4 REACHING CONSENSUS

Consensus, another intriguing word of the 1990s, was brought to our living rooms by reports about the way teams of Japanese workers make decisions. The notion of consensus is becoming an important process by which agreements are being forged today.

Consensus is the process of finding a proposal acceptable enough that all members can support it or no member can oppose it. This process can be used in all sorts of ways during negotiations, from reaching final negotiation results to deciding what items should be included on a given negotiation session's agenda.

We have used a particularly successful process as expressed in Figure 6.4 to reach consensus in our work.

This might seem an overly arduous process. We do admit that shortcuts are possible, based upon the complexity and number of the issues and the quality of previous negotiations. But the fundamental steps of listening and considering others' arguments, then working together on final proposals and agreements are "non-negotiable." As indicated in Figure 6.5, a number of key points must be considered.

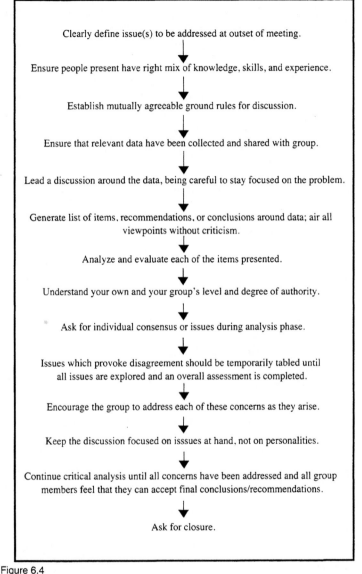

Figure 6.4

Building Consensus Process

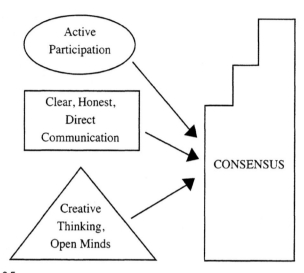

Figure 6.5

Path to Consensus

The important message here is that control of negotiations requires detailed pre-negotiation planning and vigilant monitoring as the process unfolds. A clear awareness of goals and strategic approach must be maintained. With a solid agenda, and the flexibility required to update strategies as the negotiations proceed, the negotiator can steer the process in a positive direction to achieve consensus and lay the groundwork for a successful conclusion.

A few final points on building consensus are appropriate for mention here. Building consensus requires active participation by all parties. There must be sufficient time allotted for this process to work. Clear, honest, and direct communication must exist. Creative thinking and open minds must prevail from the word go!

6.5   CONSENSUS BUILDING—AN EXAMPLE

In another negotiation we are familiar with, a major printed circuit board supplier had proposed to utilize a new manufacturing process which could reduce a price up to 40%. In discussing this possibility, the buyer in the customer's organization discovered that this price reduction was at least one year from fruition. In an attempt to reach consensus, the buyer began negotiations over a two-month period to accelerate the availability of the new process. He stressed the possibility of new and increased business, a working partnership, and a method to gain new customers. In the end, he successfully negotiated a quicker expansion of manufacturing capacity for the new process. This enabled the buyer's company to reduce board cost substantially on their own products. Consensus building can be used to achieve rich agreements benefiting both parties.

6.6   RESOLVING CONFLICT THROUGH COMMUNICATION

The essence of negotiating in teams is *effective communication* which must be regular, direct, constructive, and nonthreatening. Along with communicating effectively team members must display behavior to encourage communication. Encouraging behavior occurs when a team member:

1. Avoids feelings or perceptions which imply the other person is wrong or needs to change
2. Communicates a desire to work together to explore a problem or seek a solution
3. Exhibits behavior that is spontaneous and destruction-free
4. Identifies with another team member's problems, shares feelings, and accepts the team member's reaction
5. Treats other team members with respect and trust
6. Investigates issues rather than taking sides on them

The same principles can be applied to negotiating with others outside your team, or with a supplier or customer.

Often, there is conflict among team members. Depending on its severity, conflict can truly decimate team unity, consensus, or the ability to reach any agreement whatsoever. As the leader or key manager of the team, there are a number of actions which you could take to resolve brewing conflicts:

- Encourage the members generating the conflict to discuss the issue face to face, and away from the team setting.

- Convey the expectation that, for the benefit of the team's effort, they have a responsibility to successfully resolve the issue.
- Remind them to focus on factual issues and behaviors—not on personalities—in working to resolve their conflict.
- As a last resort, mediate the conflict yourself and require compliance with your decision.

If the conflict is between you and the team leader, use the following:

- Work directly with the individual involved in the conflict to solve the problem—in private and away from the team setting.
- Convey the expectation that, for the benefit of the team's effort, you both have a responsibility to successfully resolve the issue.
- Focus on factual issues and behaviors—not on personalities—in working to resolve the conflict.
- Demonstrate respect for the other's concerns and ideas as reflected in a genuine willingness to listen.
- Be willing to critically review your own behaviors and ideas based on the merits of the case.

Finally, if the conflict is between the team leader and the entire team, consider these actions:

- Take the initiative to discuss the conflict directly with the group as a whole—the earlier the better.
- Convey the expectation that, for the benefit of the team's effort, you all share responsibility for successfully resolving conflict.
- Focus on factual issues and behaviors—not on personalities—in working to resolve the conflict.
- Demonstrate respect for the team's concerns and ideas as reflected in a genuine willingness to listen.
- Be willing to critically review your own behaviors and ideas based on the merits of the case.

Conflict is part of life, and accordingly is part of negotiations. Some think that the stronger any negotiator's skills are in the area of resolving conflicts, the more expedient and satisfactory negotiated settlements they will achieve. So how good are your skills, and how do you stack up?

6.7   NEGOTIATING IN A HIGH-TECH ENVIRONMENT

If you are a small start-up technology company or well capitalized small technology business, you have undoubtedly sold to customers who were interested in protecting their investment. However, the tactics and terms and conditions which they attempted to negotiate with you often put your technology and therefore your company at stake. So how do you respond to these demands? What alternate proposals do you offer? How do you negotiate effectively when you are interested in securing a top prospect's business and they want you to "give away" your technology? You must use a process of negotiating which considers specific alternatives you can offer and then gain your customer's acceptance.

The Process

One of the ways to ensure that you negotiate the terms which you justly deserve is to follow a disciplined negotiating process. It has been our experience that the primary reason why negotiators of technology fail is that they attempt to reach a deal without the benefit of proper preparation, trade-off analysis, understanding of counter offers, and without possessing appropriate alternatives for agreement. We have applied a well-defined process to technologists and technology negotiators.

As you have surmised from the flowchart of our process you first must define what is to be negotiated. Ask the question: What exactly do you want to gain from the negotiation and what will you probably have to give up to achieve these results? Make a list of the key terms and aspects you want and what the customer might want in return. Define your objective in terms of what goals you want to achieve.

Some of these goals might include:

- License fees
- Patent rights
- Escrow arrangements for software
- Proprietary rights
- Documentation requirements
- Termination rights
- Training
- Technical assistance
- Customer service and spares

The Options. Some of the options for each of these areas must be thoroughly explored at the outset of your negotiation process and you must decide which are the most suitable for the particular sale you are negotiating. The following options can be evaluated.

License Fees
- Per license
- Per location
- Per company

Patent Rights Indemnity
- Within U.S. only
- Within Western countries only
- Within U.S., Europe, and Pacific Rim

Escrow Arrangements
- Upon default
- Upon bankruptcy
- Upon distribution of assets

Proprietary Rights
- Use of technology only
- Manufacturing rights
- Distribution rights

Documentation rights
- User manuals
- Manufacturing process information

- Software source codes
- Specification changes

Termination Rights
- Convenience
- Default
- Lack of sales
- Technology changes

Training
- Users
- Engineering applications
- Manufacturing staff
- Customer service representatives

Technical Assistance
- Response time
- Type and extent
- 800-number access
- Personnel access

Customer Service and Spares
- Availability
- License provisions
- Documentation requirements

Each of these options can be assigned financial values which can enable the negotiating planner to develop a carefully crafted analysis of trade-offs among these alternatives. The final result is a game plan which includes opening, fallback, and walkaway positions. Specific terms which include the aspects of the opening offer, as well as follow-up offers, should be developed.

Once developed, the terms can be proposed and evaluated by the other party. It is this testing of the plan which is essential to bring the parties closer to their true interests. Once tested and discussed, the plan can be adjusted and sold to the other party.

Packaging different alternatives is essential in the negotiating process because there is usually more than one optimal solution under which agreement can be reached. It is the job of the buyer and seller to define the various packages for consideration, then reach agreement on the best alternative which satisfies the best interests of the parties.

The Tactics. Most negotiation situations are dramatically influenced by the maturity of the product or service and the demand of the market. Depending on where a particular product or service stacks up in relation to those factors, a completely different set of strategies and tactics would need to be developed. Consider the four quadrants, each of which depicts the combination of demand and maturity that relates to a product or service, Figure 6.6.

If you are selling a new technology which provides a leading edge capability, you will probably be able to use more aggressive tactics to achieve your intended results. At this point, buyers of your product are relatively insensitive to the business terms but desire your product as quickly as you can design/make it. Buyers in this situation are in a relatively weak position due to the newness and the scarcity of the product/service.

On the other hand, if the product you are selling is relatively mature and competes with the features of other technological products, strong sales and negotiation tactics are required. You simply

Maturity

		Low	High
Demand	Low	• Emerging • Price Reasonableness • Beta Sites • Special Deals	• Features • Price and Terms Negotiation • Service
	High	• Specialized; Unique	• Commodity

Figure 6.6

Setting Negotiation Objectives based on Demand and Maturity.

must be able to package a spectacular deal for your customers, bundling terms with prices with features and service. Buyers are usually in an advantageous position due to the level of competition in the marketplace, but still might have difficulty feeling certain they receive a fair deal due to the potential complexity of the package provided.

Finally, if your product is mature, you most likely must sell on the basis of low price, as you would in the case of a commodity type product. The tactics used here, vis-à-vis competitors, could probably be described as "dog-eat-dog" and the market share of the respective companies lie in the balance. Buyers can be equally aggressive in the bargains they will pursue with the competition.

There is a point, however, that is reached when products become so mature that producing companies drop them from their product lines, leaving fewer competitors vying for a shrinking market share. Depending on the nature of the technology and the costs of maintaining a capability in that technology, the pendulum could shift into a seller's market once again.

It is extremely important to recognize which of the dimensions pertain to your products and services. Potentially, some or most of your products will fall into one of these four dimensions. Once the dimension is identified, a specific strategy can be put in place to achieve your intended results based on the options defined earlier.

Conclusion

Negotiators in the world of technology must be armed with an immense set of information and tools to negotiate effectively for their companies. First, they need a process to follow. They also must know the entire spectrum of options which pertain to their product. Third, they need to understand not only the maturity level of their products and services but also know the market demand for such products and services. This information will influence the nature of what is negotiated and the relative extent of aggressive and cooperative behavior during negotiations. Lastly, the negotiator must be able to package the needs of both parties so that an effective and efficient conclusion can be reached.

These examples demonstrate the need for creativity in maintaining control. It is important that in the planning phase, the negotiator must carefully analyze the situation to determine which approach is most likely to achieve the desired result. The bottom line, however, is that control results from aggressive efforts to achieve consensus, and effective communication.

Getting it Done:
Closing Negotiations

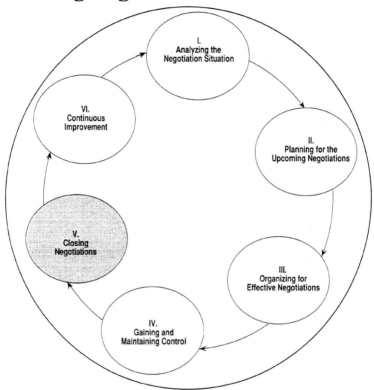

I. Analyzing the Negotiation Situation

II. Planning for the Upcoming Negotiations

III. Organizing for Effective Negotiations

IV. Gaining and Maintaining Control

V. Closing Negotiations

VI. Continuous Improvement

If you've ever been involved in a difficult negotiation and secured an acceptable agreement, you know the exhilaration of success and the immense satisfaction that all your hard work has paid off. Unfortunately, there are times when the opposite happens. Why do some negotiations succeed and others fail? Maybe we didn't exercise proper control or we didn't carefully move towards agreement. Maybe we turned off the other party.

In this chapter we address techniques of closing negotiations successfully. It is possible to negotiate and not reach agreement. This is not how we like to think about negotiation. Agreement just has to happen, the thinking goes. But failure to reach a satisfactory agreement must be accepted as a possibility as you plan for negotiations.

Some negotiators are better at reaching satisfactory agreement than others. Why? Because they use a series of techniques which make it easier for the negotiation participants to reach such an agreement. We will consider a number of these techniques in this chapter.

You can improve your chances of securing agreement in negotiations by:
- Dealing with objections
- Finding breakthroughs to gain acceptance
- Avoiding dealbreakers which throw a negotiation off course and prevent agreement
- Packaging the details into acceptable alternatives for agreement

You should also understand the nature of dealbreakers and avoid them. The effort you exert depends on the extent of possible objections, the need for creative and new solutions, and the number of possible alternatives that can be devised which can meet the requirements of the parties.

7.1   DEALING WITH OBJECTIONS

During the negotiations process a number of issues, questions, or classifications will be raised by the other party before a decision is made on whether to accept the proposal. You should plan for this in your pre-negotiations planning by raising the following questions or issues:
- Does the other party want you as a business partner?
- Are you dependable? Will you follow through on what you promise?
- Are your products or services acceptable?
- Are the terms and conditions acceptable?

- Will the other party feel satisfied if they accept?
- Will the other party be able to do better somewhere else?
- Are there any comparable alternatives available?
- Is the schedule too aggressive?
- Will any precedents be broken?

By posing these questions on your own, you will prepare to deal with them if the other party raises them during the negotiations. While it is clearly preferable that these questions and issues be answered in a positive, constructive manner, it is inevitable that some negative responses will be encountered. Such negative answers are the root of possible objections. Thus, whether the answers are favorable or unfavorable, uncovering the real objections is a useful negotiation tool because it can quickly get to the root cause of the matter.

7.2 UNCOVERING THE ROOT CAUSE

The key to resolving issues at each stage of the negotiations is to diagnose and overcome all of the objections in the other party's mind that may prevent a satisfactory answer. You must first realize that the objections being voiced may not always be the real obstacle in the deal. Therefore, it is up to you to find out what the realities of the situation are (the root causes) to bring the objections out into the open and to deal with them effectively. As objections are encountered, it may be useful to (1) clearly state your interests, (2) listen to and fully understand the other party's interests, and (3) openly invite comments, concerns, and feedback.

7.3 THE IMPORTANCE OF ATTITUDE

Your success in dealing with objections depends on your own state of mind regarding the level of trust and your willingness to negotiate with the other party. Also critical is your attitude toward the other party and toward the negotiation process in general. If you are genuinely interested in working with the other party to reach an acceptable agreement and are anxious to satisfy the other party's interests, you are far more likely to discover the root causes than if you concentrate only on the outcome or interests you hope to achieve.

If your concern is honest and sincere it will be apparent to the other party, and he or she will be more likely to talk freely with you and tell you what is unacceptable about the deal. Moreover, if your attitude convinces the other party that you really understand and care about his or her interests, any solutions you might offer are more likely to be accepted.

The attitude you convey should basically be one of openness or willingness to listen to and consider all objections. Your attitude should not reflect a desire to evade or ignore objections or be resentful toward the other party. In the view of the problem-oriented negotiator, the other party's questions, comments, and objections do not block a negotiation, but are valuable reflections of the other party's doubts, beliefs, interests, and confidence in the deal. They actually reveal the building blocks to a successful conclusion.

You should strive to be proactive rather than reactive when dealing with objections, encouraging the other party to express any reservations and reaching behind the stated objections for any additional problems. Remember, this is one aspect of building consensus. Once all of the other party's objections are out into the open, you can deal with them rationally. You thus put yourself in an excellent position to convert potential problems into settlement opportunities.

Most objections are the typical ones that are encountered in all negotiations and conflict management situations (fairness, equality, responsiveness, etc.). Over the years, negotiators have devised various ways to deal with them. Of course, some objections are of a special nature; these require special handling and considerable knowledge and flexibility on the negotiator's part. However, in all cases, the approach used should aim to secure an agreement with the other party. An example of a typical approach is indicated in Figure 7.1.

In the ongoing negotiations with Japan, it is understood that Japanese stick to original positions. Their strategy, in principle, is to "know what you want and to hold fast until you get it." We all have

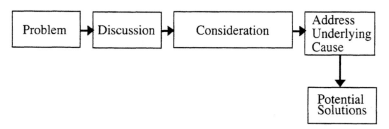

Figure 7.1
Typical Approach to Secure Agreement.

various styles in negotiations. We use different tactics. Once successful, we don't vary the plan or the approach—even if we could. We
don't focus on continuous improvement.

The Clinton Administration is trying to reverse this trend. They
have embarked on "results-oriented" strategy. Focusing on the achievement of quantitative objectives which are mutually negotiated, allows
for a change in the approach from one of adversarial to collaboration.
It is agreed that this change of approach will result in more satisfactory results.

7.4 TURNING OBJECTIONS INTO AGREEMENTS

So far we have concluded that diagnosis and overcoming objections is a big part of the overall negotiation process. During a normal
negotiation, you may have to handle numerous objections to some or
most of the following:

- Agendas
- Your own interests
- Future goals
- Location
- Timing of negotiations
- Need for data
- Extent of management involvement
- Who performs what roles?
- Fairness of solutions
- Cost/benefit analysis of alternative solutions
- Identity of lead negotiator

One of the critical tests at this juncture is to determine whether the objections of the other party are legitimate. These are some basic questions which can be asked to help determine legitimacy or concreteness:

- Is the question tied to the other party's stated interest or goals?
- Has the objection been repeatedly stated?
- Is the objection directly related to a tactic, proposal, or action taken?
- Does the objection relate to a significant amount of resources?
- Is it stated by a trustful person?
- Is the objection based upon objective criteria or reasoning?
- Can the other party back up their objection with facts and figures?
- Can the objection be ratified by a third party?

If you find that the objection cannot be rationalized then you should endeavor to "see through" the stated objection to find the real point of contention or ask the other party to justify the objection in the face of collected data.

After you determine whether the other party's objections are real, you must decide on a strategy and technique for handling them in order to maintain control of the negotiation. Once you have adequately responded to an objection, you can use the interchange to gain commitment toward some solution.

The successful handling of objections requires an intimate understanding of the other party and how he or she will react to your questions, comments, and feedback. You should state your concerns in light of the other party's needs and interests. There are some basic strategies you should follow in this regard.

1. **Avoid arguments.** Getting into an argument with the other party over an objection is one of the easiest things a negotiator can do and certainly one of the most dangerous. Place yourself in a position where you are cooperating, not conflicting with the other party.

2. **Treat all objections as reasonable and logical.** You should not treat an objection lightly just because it seems irrational or superficial to you. You should listen carefully and let the other party state his or her objection fully, even if you have heard it before or don't believe in it. This courtesy places the other party under an obligation to accord the same to you.

3. **Rephrase and repeat the objections.** This is the best starting point for handling all objections. It gives you the opportunity to ensure that you have understood the other party's objections correctly, and it may even help to clarify the issue for the other party. It also shows that you have paid attention. This is an effective active listening technique.

   By rephrasing and repeating the objection, you also gain time to think about the best way to handle it. More importantly, by turning it into a question, you can often make it easier for the other party to address.

   Don't try to guess at the reasons for the other party's objections. Your aim should be to pin down the *real* issues as rapidly as possible, and to address them. Thus, you must find the right questions to ask. Then you must present the facts that will steer the other party to answer the questions for mutual resolution.

   This technique should be used to help determine whether an objection is valid or whether it is merely an excuse, evidence of lack of planning, or even a stall.

4. **Agree with the other party or at least recognize the validity of the objection.** If you agree with any part of the objection and later counter with specific facts that will help the other party to deal with the situation differently, you can move the other party from a defensive position to a cooperative one. You have nothing to lose by agreeing that the other party's response is reasonable, logical, and worth considering. When you uncover an objection that you cannot overcome, an open admission on your part will strengthen the other party's confidence and trust in you. You would expect the same of the other party.

5. **Find any hidden objection.** This might be helpful when the other party is not objecting to anything or is being unclear as to their feelings and preferences. How do you go about uncovering hidden doubts or objections? The best technique is to ask questions that bring each objection out into the open. Keep searching for the real reason. Some questions that may be of assistance to you in uncovering hidden objections include:

  - I feel that there may be something bothering you beyond what we've discussed so far. Do you have another objection?
  - We're discussing something that could mean a great deal to both of us. What's your real feeling about this offer?
  - Why do you say that?
  - Can you get support from your organization for this type of thing?

On the other hand, we should not presume that silence means that an objection exists, and the other party is having difficulty expressing it. We should not look for trouble when none exists. We should only probe for objection when we sense that something is really wrong and getting in the way of an agreement.

By proactively dealing with objections, you can make significant strides toward reaching agreement. Be attentive to the other party's comments and reactions to your proposals and comments. Address them carefully and promptly. Failure to address objections will cause the negotiations to drag on, result in antagonistic views between the parties, and result in stalemate.

Think about the most frequent objections you encounter in negotiations. What are they? What has been your most difficult objection to respond to? How about the easiest one? How did you respond? How did the other party react? What were the results? The answers to these questions might help you design and develop appropriate countermeasures in your next negotiations.

7.5   BREAKTHROUGH THINKING

We use the word breakthrough to describe the seminal event in a negotiation in which the parties break down strong resistance and begin to gain acceptance for their proposals. By breakthroughs, we are referring to significant events, creative solutions, and innovative approaches which can transform a stalled or "event-less" negotiation into one full of promise and success. The events that these words describe are not easy to come by. To create breakthrough situations, negotiators must demonstrate creativity and innovation.

We believe that there are a number of key techniques which can be used to facilitate breakthrough thinking:

1. The negotiator should demonstrate confident nonverbal behavior in his/her activities. This means that he/she should exude confidence in greetings, closings, and overall behavior.
2. The negotiator must listen and constructively react to the other party's responses.
3. Each party should help the other "save face."
4. The negotiator should use questions to show interest and support.
5. The negotiator should step back to ensure that the solutions being considered are the best possible for both parties. The best way to do this is to put yourself in the other party's position and ask the question: Is this the best solution for us? How can we change to better achieve our goals? Can I sell this solution once I return to the office?

7.6   MAKING BREAKTHROUGHS HAPPEN

Breakthroughs

Breakthroughs are turning points that lead to settlements. They do not just happen, they occur because negotiators look for opportunities to accommodate each other's interest and seek creative solutions. Although breakthroughs can result from joint efforts, frequently one party's proactive efforts to break impasses are enough to get the process going.

We have observed many situations in which a creative suggestion resolved seemingly irreconcilable differences. Here are examples
seen in differing negotiations:

Buying

- Offer long term contract in exchange for price concession.
- Provide tooling to keep supplier's cost down.
- Pay higher price in exchange for exclusive use of product or
  proprietary rights.
- Offer value engineering, engineering support, or quality con-
  trol people to ensure economical production.
- Offer to train supplier's people.

Selling

- Throw in extras; i.e., optional features, extended warranties,
  reduced financing costs.
- House sale—include furniture, appliances, deeded beach
  rights, country club membership, financing assistance, etc.
- Offer lower price for long-term relationship.
- Schedule high-level meeting between bosses to determine
  mutual interest and how each side can help.

Leases

- Sign longer lease for reduced rent.
- Waive security deposits or accept short-term lease.
- Propose no payments for first six months, year, etc.
- Offer free services, maintenance, cleaning, etc.

Labor Disputes

- Exchange benefits for wage demand reductions or benefit
  give-backs for wage increases.
- Offer employee ownership.

- Intervention by third party, such as a high government official
- Modifiy work rules, flexible time, reduced work week, etc.

Government-to-Government

- Remove trade sanctions or threat to impose sanctions.
- Offer to assist in conversion from wartime to peacetime.
- Allow on-site inspection to ascertain compliance to terms.
- Display overwhelming force to induce acceptance of terms (e.g., Hiroshima and Nagasaki).
- Offer to drop threat to use force in exchange for concessions (e.g., Cuban Missile Crisis).
- Make precedent-breaking offer to meet with historic enemy and begin negotiations (Camp David accords).

All of these breakthroughs (except for the Hiroshima example) occurred because one of the parties made an offer which included some benefit to the other side, thus creating a spirit of concession.

An interesting breakthrough technique was employed during the Cuban Missile Crisis in October 1962. In that situation, Russian long-range nuclear missiles had been discovered by U.S. reconnaissance flights over Cuba. Since these missiles posed a threat to U.S. cities, negotiations to remove them were immediately begun by the White House. Over a ten-day period, the U.S. imposed a blockade of Cuba and exchanged with the Soviets various ideas for defusing the crisis. Toward the end of negotiations, the Russians cabled a particularly harsh message which raised the stakes so that a nuclear war seemed possible. As U.S. officials struggled with a proper response to the Russian demands, the president's brother, Robert Kennedy, suggested that the U.S. reply ignore the tougher Russian message and act as if it had never been received. Since the Russians apparently preferred not to have sent it, both parties returned to the previous lower level of intensity and negotiations continued to a successful conclusion and war was avoided.

This is an example of helping the opposition step back from an extremely volatile position. It helps your opponent to "save face" and helps to break through an impasse.

7.7 PERSONAL CONSIDERATIONS

In any negotiation, the personal interests of the negotiators are bound to be a factor, despite the advice of many experts that the focus should be on issues rather than personalities. Personal considerations impact situations in various ways. For example, the negotiator can lose objectivity by becoming agitated over a negative development, and lose control of the situation causing disastrous results. We are aware of many cases, particularly where personal and financial considerations are involved, in which negotiators have lost sight of primary strategic goals because of a perceived insult and walked away in anger. Usually, disaster follows such behavior. We recognize that it is very difficult to keep control of a situation where high personal stakes are involved. But control can be maintained with steel resolve and an awareness of the other party's use of unsettling tactics.

An interesting case involved a colleague of ours who was negotiating the sale of his small, essentially one-man, company with a large firm. The deal was crucial to his future financial well-being so our colleague was nervous as he approached the negotiations. The large firm had secured the services of an attorney, who was a professional negotiator to represent them in the matter. As the negotiation began, the lawyer (whom our friend dubbed the "hired gun") noted our friend's nervousness and offered to get him a soft-drink. The "hired gun" poured the drink into a paper cup, filling it to the brim. As he raised the cup, our friend spilled the contents onto the paper work he had brought to the table. He was very unnerved but realized his opponent had deliberately set him up for the embarrassment. At that point, he stood up, accused the attorney of unprofessional conduct and broke off the negotiations. He suggested that the lawyer tell his client that if they would send someone to represent them in a professional ethical manner, he would agree to talk to them. At the next meeting, our friend achieved an acceptable result.

This case provides two lessons regarding the personal involvement of negotiators. First, some negotiators attempt to capitalize on an opponent's personal involvement to gain a tactical advantage. Secondly, it is important for a negotiator to recognize a destructive tactic when it is employed, to defuse it as soon as possible, and to turn it back on the opponent so that it backfires.

Personal factors can also have a positive effect on a negotiation. An example is the recognition of our opponent's personal stake in a negotiation and how this can be a factor in win/win conclusions. By considering what the opponent needs or desires to achieve, the negotiator becomes much more creative in finding solutions which respond to each party's objectives. From this kind of thinking, visionary conclusions can be reached, not only creating a successful result but laying the foundation for beneficial relationships in the future.

7.8   BRAINSTORMING ALTERNATIVES

Brainstorming techniques can also be used to determine other possible solutions. This technique is useful when there are outspoken members of either party who are dominating the discussion, when the parties have not negotiated with each other before, or when the parties want to ensure that everyone has a voice in potential solutions. As depicted in Figure 7.2, the brainstorming process is very straightforward.

The most frequent way to begin to generate ideas is to ask each member of the negotiation group to suggest one idea in a prescribed sequence and then continue to follow the sequence until all ideas are exhausted. Brainstorming goes a long way to ensure that all viewpoints are considered.

Among other techniques to consider in developing breakthroughs is the conduct of dry-run negotiation sessions. You could also present your proposals to peers or uninvolved observers for independent assessment and input. You should always test for reasonableness by asking the question: Is this a fair and reasonable solution for both parties which satisfies their respective interests?

7.9   DEALBREAKERS

Just as there are turning points for the better in negotiations, there are also those actions or maneuvers that destroy the atmosphere, produce ill will on both sides, and eliminate the possibility of agreement. These events often result from a tactic that backfires, or discourages, or even humiliates the other party so that momentum toward an agreement is interrupted and negotiations broken off.

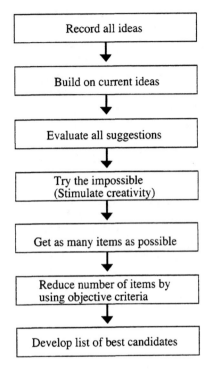

Figure 7.2

The Brainstorming Process

We refer to these happenings as dealbreakers, because they often prevent agreements, sometimes turning apparent success into failure. Here are some examples of moves that we have seen prove destructive:

- A very low offer by a buyer, after earnest efforts by the seller to be reasonable had produced apparent progress.
- A move by one party to exacerbate the conflict after negotiations had begun. One example is revoking an established benefit or privilege that was not part of the disagreement at issue, thus raising the stakes and moving the parties further

apart. Such an offensive move is usually made to "get their attention" but it frequently sours the mood and is counter-productive. Everyone must now work twice as hard to get back on track.

This tactic was employed in the 1994 major league baseball dispute. Almost immediately after the players went on strike, the owners announced that an $8 million payment to the players' retirement fund would not be made, despite a previous commitment to do so. This contributed to a very bitter dispute which covered the cancellation of the last two months of the 1994 season and at this writing has not yet been settled, threatening the entire season of 1995.

- After a struggle to reach agreement, one party loses temper and states that he'd rather "lose everything than yield one penny to the other party." In one reported example of this lack of control, a huge development project, in which each side had a very large investment, fell apart because the intemperate party walked out. The other party sued for breach of contract and won triple damages in the amount of $150 million.

- Who hasn't had the experience of agreeing on a price with a car salesperson only to be told at the last minute that the deal had to be approved by the sales manager? When the price is then raised by the boss, the disgusted customer walks out.

It will be wise in our planning to give some thought to potential deal breakers that might occur. Such happenings can be prevented by posing the following questions:

- What are they?
- Who would possibly suggest them?
- Why would they be offered?
- How might you counter such a development?
- How might you pre-sell your best solution to forestall any objections or dealbreakers?

7.10 ASSESSING THE LEVEL OF SUPPORT FOR A PROPOSED SOLUTION

We have developed a tool to assist in assessing the level of support that various members of our own and the other party might have, relative to our proposal. This tool, described in Figure 7.3, provides a baseline to help determine the key supporters and opponents who must be either won over or enlisted on our search for winning solutions.

The last step of this process which addresses the proactive steps or plans you will take, is a critical piece of the process. It creates a closed loop from diagnosis of the level of support to the actions required to maximize the chance that the proposal will be adopted. Oftentimes there is diagnosis or recognition of a problem but solutions are written off as superfluous or due to a breakdown in communications. Our point here is that the only way to respond to the level of support you have is to assess it, then decide whether to pursue a different course if need be, or immediately put plans in place to build support. By using some of these tools, you will build support for your breakthrough ideas.

7.11 PACKAGING THE DETAILS OF THE NEGOTIATION

One of the primary obstacles faced by negotiators when they attempt to reach agreement on the best solution is that each party has their "one and only" or sole solution which they profess spreads the most benefits among the parties. To address this, we advocate the development of a number of different solutions which can satisfy both of the parties. This range of alternatives will most likely include the initial or preferred solution of both parties. Much like the funnel used in selecting which new products a given company might invest in, the solution funnel (see Figure 7.4) evaluates each of the potential solutions against a set of criteria agreed upon by the parties. This down-select process results in a few (probably not more than three) possible packages of options, features, terms and conditions, and provisions which can be acceptable to the parties.

1) List individuals attending meeting

    a. _____

    b. _____

    c. _____

    d._____

Rate on scale of 1-5 on support of proposal (1 = against, 5 = for)

2) Single out opposition

    • Who?
    • Why?
    • Evaluate reasons

3) Single out supporters

    • Who?
    • Why?
    • Evaluate reasons

Focus: Examine the goal, the level of support, and reasons for support/lack of support.

4) Devise ways to create more support for proposal.

Figure 7.3

Assessment Tool to Evaluate Support

The general rules to follow are to first sort the issues to be negotiated into two piles—those which can be packaged and those which have to be dealt with on an individual basis. Try to reduce or eliminate the stand-alone issues. Combine as many issues as possible into natural groupings of balanced solutions. Identify individual or stand-alone issues needing resolution. Then determine the stand-alone solution and present it as part of a combined package. It might be helpful to combine issues so that solutions need not deal with minutiae.

Thus the packaging process can be portrayed as indicated in Figure 7.5.

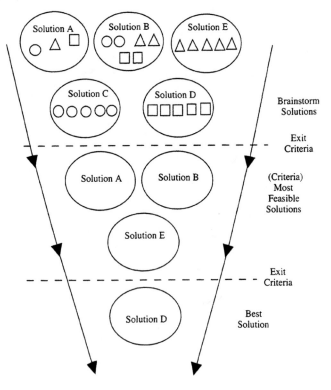

Figure 7.4

The Solution Funnel

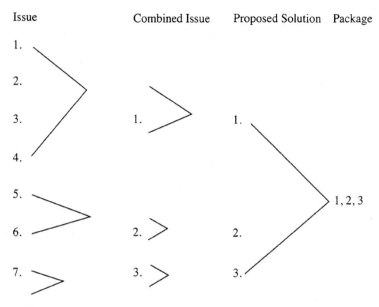

Figure 7.5

Packaging Negotiation Solutions

This process is analogous to buying a computer. Think about what features you want to bundle together. It is useful to develop a minimum and maximum outcome for each negotiable item or "feature" as well as a probable outcome. Can you live with the probable outcome? How can you be innovative to overcome the resistance or obstacles from the other party? What do you need to do to sell it in favorable terms to the other party?

These questions and more must be considered as you attempt to reach a favorable conclusion. We all want to be successful. It is our experience that working together with the other party to develop various packages of options, including breakthrough items, will provide the best opportunity for you to reach a sustainable result! Finally, don't be afraid to be creative and innovative. It is the absence of these aspects and the reliance on precedence which kill the prospect of satisfactory negotiations.

Getting it Done: Continuous Improvement—Techniques to Improve Negotiation Performance

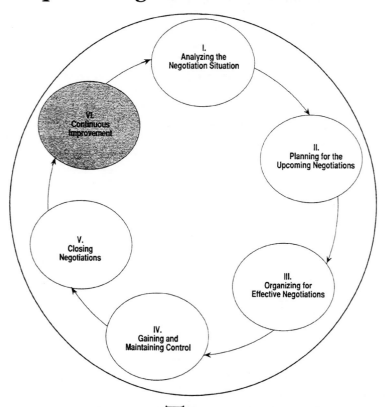

The notions of continuous improvement, TQM, and re-engineering have taken the business world by storm. Why? The basic concept—understanding processes used in accomplishing work so that each element of the process can be analyzed for optimization and efficiency—can have a dramatic impact on organizations where innovation has been kept in check. We believe that the concept can be successfully applied to negotiations.

First of all, negotiation is a process. That is what this book has been about. We have described six major steps which we advocate to be used in any negotiating situation. Within each step there are additional substeps to be completed. For example, to *define* what is to be negotiated, the negotiator must evaluate the environment, then review the constraints being discussed, and then establish the particular broad goals for the negotiation.

Substeps each have a "customer," someone who receives the information from the substep, uses the data, or is influenced in some way by the actual accomplishment of the substep itself. By asking the customers to define their needs, one is able to structure an approach to the work and a procedure for measuring results. This allows the negotiator to report on what he/she has negotiated and receive the customer's feedback and concerns. Examples of these types of customers include the following:

- The party with whom you are negotiating
- The department within your company for whom you are negotiating
- The ultimate users of the products or services you are procuring
- Your boss or family member

If you do what others are expecting at the outset of negotiations, then you can measure how well their needs have been satisfied. Once the negotiator has determined the various needs of the parties and has structured a reasonable game plan for the negotiations, then it is highly recommended that this individual be empowered to complete the negotiations with minimal involvement from management or more senior or experienced individuals.

If we combine these four aspects of continuous improvement, we can begin to develop a context for discussion and evaluation about how to apply these aspects to completed or partially completed negotiations as follows:

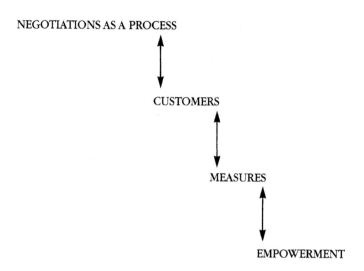

NEGOTIATIONS AS A PROCESS

8.1 REVIEW THE PROCESS

Contrast the process you have used in accomplishing your negotiations with the one espoused in this book or another process which
you believe is successful, then ask the following questions:

- Which steps were missed?
- Which steps were not necessary?
- Which steps added value to the process?
- Did the worthwhile steps take too long? Why or why not?
- Did you employ another step which proved to be effective?
- How realistic were your expectations about whether the
  other party was willing to follow this process versus another?

The reason for asking these questions is to evaluate the process
used, its strong and weak points, and determine how to improve the
process the next time. As graphically protrayed in Figure 8.1, the best
way to do this is to determine the largest gap between what is
requested from the negotiation process and what was achieved.

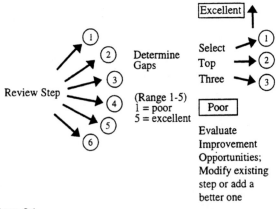

Figure 8.1

Gap Analysis

8.2 TALK WITH CUSTOMERS

During the planning stages of negotiations, you would have discussed the needs of your internal customers. Based upon these discussions, you would have developed goals and negotiation objectives that were reflective of your customer's needs. At various stages of the negotiations, you probably would have provided status reports to these customers on an ongoing basis. If you have followed this process you would be in excellent shape to evaluate whether you were able to satisfy their needs. If you haven't, perhaps you have partially completed some of the key steps so the stakeholders' objectives can be discerned from the strategy. If not, all you will be left with is either the strategy itself or the negotiation results.

Stakeholder	Objectives	Results	Shortfall
1.	_____	_____	_____
2.	_____	_____	_____
3.	_____	_____	_____
4.	_____	_____	_____
5.	_____	_____	_____

Figure 8.2

Objectives Grid

This evaluation can start anywhere on the grid (Figure 8.2). To determine how successful you have been in completed negotiations, ask the following questions:

- Were the customers satisfied? Why or why not?
- Where was I able to meet customer expectations? Not meet them?
- How have the results of the negotiations impacted the customers in a positive way? In a negative way?
- What are the customer's expectations for the next set of negotiations?
- How might I change the following aspects of negotiations to better serve the customer? Use the following template:

<table>
<tr><td></td><td>Change Required</td></tr>
<tr><td>•• Up-front Planning</td><td>_____</td></tr>
<tr><td></td><td>_____</td></tr>
<tr><td></td><td>_____</td></tr>
<tr><td>•• Approach to Overall Negotiation</td><td>_____</td></tr>
<tr><td></td><td>_____</td></tr>
<tr><td></td><td>_____</td></tr>
<tr><td>•• Time Spent with Customers</td><td>_____</td></tr>
<tr><td></td><td>_____</td></tr>
<tr><td></td><td>_____</td></tr>
<tr><td>•• Negotiation Tactics</td><td>_____</td></tr>
<tr><td></td><td>_____</td></tr>
<tr><td></td><td>_____</td></tr>
<tr><td>•• Selection of Alternatives
   for Solutions</td><td>_____</td></tr>
<tr><td></td><td>_____</td></tr>
<tr><td>•• Way of Reaching Consensus
   on Final Outcome(s)</td><td>_____</td></tr>
<tr><td></td><td>_____</td></tr>
</table>

By assessing the feedback received from customers as to whether you met their expectations, you can address each concern head-on and improve your approach and style appropriately.

8.3   MEASURING YOUR NEGOTIATION RESULTS

If you prepared for negotiation in the fashion we have been advocating, you will have quantitative measures to compare with your negotiation results. For example, if you ended up in our real estate example paying $160,000 for the house, this can be directly compared with either the walk-away figure in the plan or your "most probable" outcome.

Plan		Results	Reasons for Outcome
Best	$155,000		_____
Most Likely	$157,500		_____
		$160,000	
Walk-Away	$162,500		_____

Using this format, you could describe the specifics as to why you paid an amount close to your walk-away figure and far away from your initial position. You might have experienced difficulty in quanlitative measurements of some of the objectives such as:

- *A Long-Term Relationship*
  Measure quality of terms and conditions, management, commitment, or duration
- *Win/Win Results*
  Based on both party's perceptions, or established *joint* ventures
- *Quality Products and Services*
  Focus on reliability, percent failures, customer satisfaction
- *Joint Development*
  Level of involvement, extent of communication, degree of management participation and resources (physical, technical, financial) committed

Although these types of objectives are more difficult to measure and evaluate, appropriate measures can be developed so that results can be objectively assessed. Once the data is available, ask the following questions:

1. How significant were the gaps in achievement? Why?
2. Were some objectives over-achieved at the expense of others? If yes, which ones? Why?
3. Were the initial objectives unmeasureable? If yes, which ones? Why did this happen? Too low, too high?

In our research, we did hear from a few negotiators in companies where "target" prices were established without participation from key inputs such as purchasing, engineering, or manufacturing. How realistic can these targets be? More companies would benefit in accomplishing internal target negotiations first, so that there would be more buy-in and empowerment by the participants in the negotiation. Don't just focus on unrealistically *high* objectives, worry about the unrealistically low ones as well. Both result in suboptimal negotiations.

At the end of WWII, the United States allowed Emperor Hirohito to remain on the scene in Japan. Some would argue (quite vehemently) that the U.S. and the Allies suboptimized their negotiation results by not insisting on criminal proceedings or expulsion! The post-war history of our relations with Japan vindicates the wisdom of the magnanimous approach. We are sure that by scrutinizing the long-term effects of past negotiations, similar conclusions would be reached.

8.4   EVALUATE EXTENT OF NEGOTIATION EMPOWERMENT

Empowerment is the current buzz-word for employee involvement. It embodies the notion that people take the responsibility and authority, as well as the tools to manage their work, with a minimal level of management involvement. You wouldn't necessarily wish to "empower" an inexperienced person to perform work outside their sphere of knowledge, but for more experienced personnel this is the wave of the future. The current thinking is, allow the brainpower closest to the work to plan, accomplish, and evaluate its own work. In the area of negotiations, this would be applicable in:

1. The way negotiators are required to seek approvals for their negotiation plans

2. The ability of the negotiator(s) to change their negotiation plan during the negotiations process without management approval
3. The degree that the negotiator(s) can represent the interests of an organization or individual(s)
4. The requirement for updating negotiation status and progress
5. The level of responsibility and accountability given to the negotiator(s) regarding results

Figure 8.3 contains an assessment of the degree of empowerment that often exists for various aspects of a negotiation.

Level of Empowerment	Scale of 1-5 (1= low; 5= excellent)
Planning	2
Strategy	2
Tactics	3
Accountability	5

Figure 8.3

Empowerment Scale

Now how can that be? How can the negotiators be completely accountable for negotiation results when the very plans, strategies, and tactics (to a lesser extent) are being dictated or specified by third parties? Obviously they cannot and shouldn't be measured in this fashion. We should give the negotiator(s) the authority to set objectives and develop plans based on customer input and then allow the negotiator(s) to effect negotiations without substantial intervention by management or the principal stakeholders.

8.5   ESTABLISHING THE BASELINE: APPLYING THE TOOLS

The analysis of these four factors—process, customers, measures, and empowerment—provides a baseline of performance set against the expected results from the negotiations. Ranges in performance can be readily identified and assessed, so that informed and formal action plans can be put into effect to improve the outcomes of future negotiations.

To do this effectively, many companies have used versions of the Plan-Do-Check-Act (PDCA) tool, originally developed by Walter Shewart. This four-step process allows the negotiator to develop changes in how he/she plans for, approaches, and uses a negotiation process, and selects and uses tactics and styles in negotiations. It allows him/her to make the change, try it out in an upcoming negotiation, evaluate results achieved and then take actions to further modify the approach on standardizing the behavior or activity for all future negotiations.

8.6   ISO-9000 NEGOTIATIONS:
BETWEEN BUYERS AND SELLERS

Since the late 1980s, the words "ISO-9000" have been in the minds and hearts of many U.S. manufacturers, suppliers, managers, and quality consultants. The ISO-9000 series of quality management and quality assurance standards were developed by a technical committee working under the auspices of the International Standards Organization (ISO). The initial standards were released in 1987 and were revised in 1994. The ISO-9000 series include five (5) subsections:

- ISO-9000–Guidelines for use of the four ISO standards
- ISO-9001–Guidelines for the design, production, installation, and servicing of products
- ISO-9002–Guidelines for production and installation of product
- ISO-9003–Guidelines for final inspection and testing of products
- ISO-9004–Guidelines for managers of an organization to help them in building their quality system.

These standards are quality guidelines which can be used to control the day-to-day management of companies that make products and even provide services to their customers. Since its predecessor standards, BSO-5750, were developed, over 30,000 sites in Europe

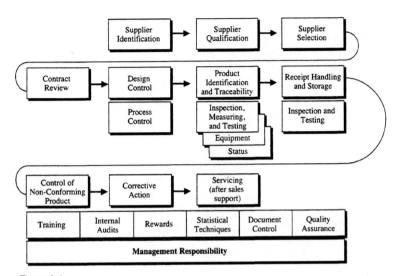

Figure 8.4

Quality System

have been certified or registered to following these guidelines. As of the writing of this book, over 2,500 sites in the United States have been registered. Both of these sets of guidelines include the flow of activities indicated in Figure 8.4.

Why do companies choose to become registered to the ISO-9000 series? The reasons range from forcing a level of quality standardization in their companies to representing a type of recognition for a particular plant's or site's quality procedures and operating procedures. Many companies choose to pursue ISO-9000 registration as a result of their customers' request to be a "certified" or "approved" supplier. Some large U.S. companies, like Motorola and IBM, are requiring their suppliers to become registered so that they can receive future orders. ISO-9000 is becoming a recognized standard of performance, to which companies can be compared vis-à-vis other companies in their field. Companies are becoming registered to be on the business "playing field." Oftentimes buyers negotiate the need and schedule of registration for a specific ISO-9000 series. The various objectives of both parties are described in the following table:

Buyer	Seller
• Create a standard for certification	• Demonstrate its commitment to quality
• Reduce its supplier base	• Receive recognition for its more accomplished sites
• Ensure purchases made are from the best suppliers	• Become one of a short list of certified suppliers.

When negotiating the aspects of ISO-9000 implementation, buyers and sellers would most likely include the following items in negotiation discussions:

1. Standard to pursue (9001, 9002, or 9003)
2. Registrar to use
3. Domestic or international applicability
4. Numbers of sites
5. Schedule for completion
6. Outcomes of registration
7. Effect of registration on seller's ability to receive additional business from buyer
8. Business activities or functions important to buyers

Sellers who decide to pursue the ISO series will also need to negotiate with internal staff and potential registrars. Internal staff must be willing to manage the project, assign staff, become trained, manage the process, and deliver on the ISO-9000 registration as agreed with the customer. The steps to implementation are significant and will include those listed below:

- The preparation of quality plans and a corporate quality manual in accordance with the specified requirements
- The identification and acquisition of any controls, processes, inspection equipment, fixtures, total production resources, and skills that may be needed to achieve the required quality
- The updating, as necessary, of company quality control, including inspection, testing techniques, and the development of new instrumentation and gauges

- The identification of any measurement requirement involving capability that exceeds the known state of the art in sufficient time for the needed capability to be developed
- The clarification of standards of acceptability for all features and requirements, including those which contain a subjective element
- The compatibility of the design, the production process, installation, inspection and test procedures, and the applicable specifications related to subcontractor-furnished products and services
- The identification and preparation of quality records

These steps can easily fit into a process-flow time-line as indicated in Figure 8.5.

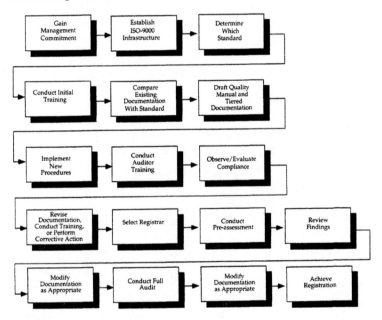

Figure 8.5

ISO-9000 Registration Process

A number of these steps are directly negotiated with the external registrar, an independent assessor who reviews the company's quality manual and quality documentation, conducts on-site audits, and provides feedback on performance. Fees will need to be agreed upon, ultimate schedule of preliminary and formal audits must be established, as well as the key requirements for registration.

For those companies which have gone through the ISO-9000 registration process, a constant set of negotiations could be undertaken, including sub-suppliers and their suppliers, as reflected in Figure 8.6.

Since ISO-9000 registrars take on the average about 18 months; these negotiations are regular, specific, and very purposeful. In fact, failure to manage these negotiations effectively will result in less than optimal performance or lower customer satisfaction.

The Plan-Do-Check-Act (PDCA) tool exhibited in Figure 8.7 is used in all sorts of problem solving and empowerment activities, and it can be effective in structuring an action plan to be implemented for improving negotiations over and over again.

We work from the premise that even the best negotiator can improve over the long term . . . . no one is perfect and accordingly everyone can improve. We remember the old joke about the New Yorker, who, when asked, "How do you get to Carnegie Hall?" replied, "Practice!" It is true for concert pianists, baseball players, spelling bee participants, and computer users that the more you *practice, train,* and *want to improve,* the better you become. We vividly remember

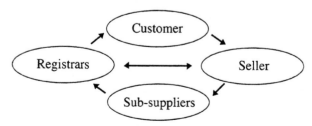

Figure 8.6

Tying Buyers and Sellers Together under ISO Registration

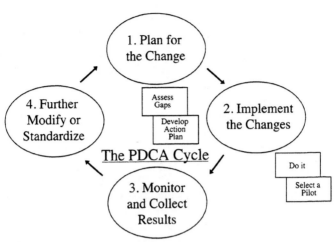

Figure 8.7

Detailed PDCA Cycle

basketball great Larry Bird, practicing for two solitary hours in an empty arena during a championship series, after receiving the Most Valuable Player award earlier that day. Use this philosophy to accomplish your negotiation objectives. Be a career negotiator. Develop yourself through self training, independent reading, and practice. And finally, in today's world, ensure that all parties feel good about the results at the end of it all!!!

Using the
Six-Step Approach

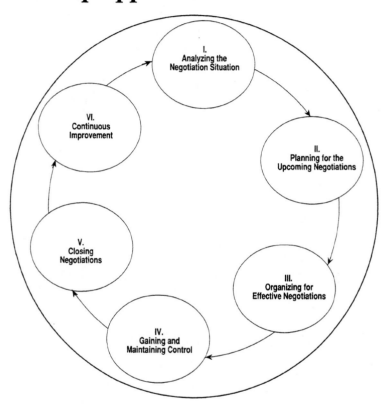

We have attempted to describe the approach in such a way that you might be able to easily implement it the next time you attempt to negotiate. We have included many templates and questions which can be used to apply the approach. Numerous examples have also been part of the material.

So that you may apply the approach even more directly after reading this book, we offer the material in this section. What we have set out to do is to put you in the shoes of a negotiator. We have also used the various forms and formats suggested in the material so that they may "come alive" for you. Finally, we ask you to make some of the choices so that you may see the ramifications of the choices made.

In the balance of this section, then, is a case study on negotiations. In it, you will be asked to play the role of the lead or key negotiator, one who makes the important decisions and is the primary contributor in representing your party's interests at the negotiating sessions.

9.1   NEGOTIATION SITUATION DATA

You are about to negotiate a major purchase. Most people define a major purchase to be a car, a house, a piece of equipment, a renovation of a kitchen, or services such as house painting or roof repair. We are all confronted with these types of purchases and the related negotiations during the course of our work or personal life.

Let's assume that you have determined that a *purchase* is required and you have access to the available funds. Now let's work through each step of our process.

Step 1: Analyzing the Negotiation Situation

Depending on the nature of the industry or community you find yourself in, the environment could be either buyer- or seller-based. A buyer's market is one where the buyer's purchasing power is superior to the seller's ability to control prices, schedules, and terms. Thus, as of the writing of this book, the environment would look like this:

Situation Market	Leverage
Real Estate	Buyer's
Car Purchase	Mostly Buyer's
Renovations	Mostly Buyer's
Major Equipment	Buyer's

This data tells us that the buyer has the upper hand in setting the terms. Of course, there are exceptions. For instance, in some desirable neighborhoods, it may be difficult to find the configuration you have in mind. In some automobiles, all the options may not be available for in-stock vehicles. Chances are that there is little precedent for such purchases, unless someone you know has purchased a similar product, house, or service and has provided information on their experience.

Goals must be established. Fill in the blanks in Figure 9.1.

1. Not to Exceed Price to be Paid   _____

2. Absolutely Required   _____
   Features (not negotiable)   _____

3. Absolutely Required   _____
   Terms (i.e., payment)   _____

4. Other Goals:

        Yes / No

   Foster long-term relationship   _____

   Gain commitment from seller   _____

   Get schedule of delivery set   _____

   Set up communication channel
      for future requirements   _____

Figure 9.1

Statement of Negotiating Goals

You should also research the other party and determine their sense of urgency, potential goals, perception of your side's interests, internal costs, preferred seating arrangements, and the personalities of the party. You should evaluate the extent to which you have options to negotiate with different parties. This is very true when you buy a car but is less true or nonexistent when you buy a specialized piece of equipment. This information can then be summarized into a working document as you enter Step 2 of the process.

Step 2: Planning for the Upcoming Negotiations

In Step 1, we researched the other party. We learned what motivated them, and their general goals and expectations. We were also able to delineate our own goals. The key task in Step 2 is to define the interests of both parties. These should be stated explicitly and ranked from most to least important.

Our Interests (Buyer)	Their Interests (Seller)
• Price < 15K	• Price > 14 K
• Delivery	• Warranty Option
• Features	• Features
• Free Service	• Delivery
• Free A/C	
• Warranty Options	

In the above example of a car purchase, we find that the only common interests, in terms of acceptance, are prices and features. As can be noted, there are other common interests but these are weighed differently. There are also different interests. All of the interests must be examined for compatibility and whether they can be played off on one another during negotiations. For example, pricing might be higher if delivery can be expedited, or warranty options can be conceded if free service is offered for the first 12 months.

The strengths and weaknesses of each party's interest should be gauged and assessed at this point. That is, determine who has the advantage in terms of:
  • Environment
  • Procedures

- Stake in results
- Time
- Information
- Power

Assign pluses or minuses to describe your relative position. Assess the negatives and find ways to turn them into positives or work with the other party to share equally in each area. Once this analysis is done, then you should establish reasonable objectives or those quantifiable aspects of the negotiations which satisfy the goals.

Objectives for a perspective home purchase could be:
- Pay no more than $150,000 with an 8% rate in 30 years
- Pay no more than $155,000 with a 7-1/2 % rate over 30 years
- Include all white goods in purchase price
- Set up closing date within 60 days
- Seller performs inspection and pest evaluation at no cost to buyer
- Seller fixes screens on porch before closing.

We suggest that most, if not all, of these objectives be shared with the seller except perhaps the offer price. You could even address these areas by stating, "We are prepared to offer $150,000 unless your real estate agent can arrange a lower interest rate, in which case we might be willing to offer a different price." The other party should be expected to share their objectives as well. Once this occurs, the parties can compare the two sets of objectives and evaluate where there is room for negotiation and where there could be potential trade-offs.

Step 3: Organizing for Effective Negotiations

Once the objectives have been evaluated and the relative strengths of the parties have been analyzed, then a game plan should be established. This game plan would include a negotiation strategy which would describe how offers and counter offers will be made, how the team's roles and responsibilities will be delineated, what is planned with respect to the number of negotiation sessions, when negotiations will take place, and how the progress of the negotiation will be statused, used, or maintained.

We suggest using the template indicated in Figure 9.2 for this activity.

- Roles and Responsibilities:

		Us	The other Party
••	Recorder	___	___
••	Time Keeper	___	___
••	Social Director	___	___
••	Leader	___	___

- Number of Sessions:

			Us	The other Party
••	Timing:	This week	___	___
		This month	___	___
		This quarter	___	___
		This year	___	___

- Location of Negotiations:

Initial	___
Final	___

- Offer and Counter Offer Information:

Item	Initial	Fallback	Walkaway
___	___	___	___
___	___	___	___
___	___	___	___
___	___	___	___

- How status of negotiation will be reported:

Verbal	_____
In writing	_____
Combination	_____

Figure 9.2

Negotiation Template

Be prepared to adjust your plan based on new information, new ideas becoming available, or competitor initiatives.

Step 4: Taking Control

The agenda for the first negotiation session should be established. A draft copy of the agenda should be circulated or communicated to the other party for comment, or in the cases of car and house buying, the agenda items can be agreed upon at the outset of each negotiation session.

Once negotiations are under way, the negotiator can test the viability of the plan in terms of:

- Acceptability by the other party
- The coverage of all appropriate issues and concerns
- The inclusion of all roles and responsibilities
- The efficacy of the time constraints

The key here is to be ready and willing to change your plan if it is clearly not working and you've done your best to implement it. As negotiations continue, the trick is to test and adjust, as shown in Figure 9.3.

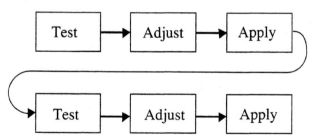

Figure 9.3

Test/Apply Process

In the case of the car purchase, this would look like:

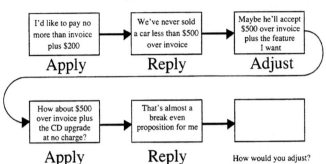

Figure 9.4

Test/Apply Process Application

This obviously goes back and forth. Perhaps the buyer increases his price or lowers his expectations. Maybe the seller will counter offer including another option for consideration (one that probably doesn't cost him as much). Ultimately, the individual who is able to reach a consensus with the other party will also be able to continue negotiations in spite of a number of disagreements. Counterproposals will then push the negotiations toward closure. This is more likely to occur if control is maintained.

Step 5: Closing Negotiations

The key to successful closure is the creation of an agreement which is packaged in a way that both sides can accept. As we saw in the car negotiation example above, a number of packages can be offered to satisfy each party's objectives. One could look at the total cost of the transaction to determine the value of any given alternative. To do this, an attempt must be made to quantify each element of the counter offers made. For example, note the differences in offers and the similarities in the final costs in the example below.

New Home Example (Value to Buyer)

	#1	#2	#3
Offer Price	$150,000	$154,000	$157,750
Inspection Costs Included	750	750	
Remodeling/ Problems Corrected	2,250		
White Goods Included	1,750		
Rental Income on Existing Property Included			(-3,000)
TOTAL	$154,750	$154,750	$154,750

Figure 9.5

Home Negotiation Outcomes

The point here is that the offer packages are completely different, and at least three options are available if either party is interested in providing the buyer with a "value" of $154, 750. As you keep the negotiation controlled through agendas and implementation of your plan, ensure that everyone is focused toward the identified common objective:

- To sell you a car at a reasonable price
- To give you fair market value for your house
- To provide the best value to you for the features offered

If you see anyone in either party straying from the objective, be sure to bring then immediately back in focus. Find out who supports your willingness to buy (in this example):

Negotiable Item	Best Candidate for Support
Car Purchase	Salesperson, dealer, manager
House Purchase	Most sentimental
Equipment Purchase	Salesperson, not district manager

Identify things that can help package the deal. Figure out how to influence others to your way of thinking, whether it be based on total costs, tradeoffs on features, or based on future purchases. Then seek acceptance by fully carrying out your plan. Look for signs of agreement like, "I'd like to sell to you, but . . . we still have a minor pricing problem," etc.

Step 6: Continuous Improvement

Once you have completed negotiations, do some introspection. Review the original goals and interest statements. Flow chart the recently completed negotiations, from start to finish. Identify where major problems were encountered. Answer the following questions and learn from the results:

1. Were your own needs and the other negotiator's needs fulfilled?
2. Did you plan and prepare properly? What did you overlook? What did you learn?
3. What styles did you employ and when?
4. What tactics were used; how did they work?
5. Were your objectives set too high or low? Were they reasonable?
6. Did you use time effectively?
7. How did you communicate; was it successful?
8. How did you use language; did it have an impact on the result of the negotiations?

Perhaps you didn't research the other party properly. That might have resulted in surprises and displays of power. Maybe the other party really didn't want to negotiate. This would have caused delays and resulted in frustration in your part.

The purpose of evaluating what happened is to identify problems to assess the quality of the response you made, to learn from how your response either positively or negatively affected the negotiation, and to create some explicit or implicit rules which you will follow *the next time*. This is how learning occurs (see Figure 9.6).

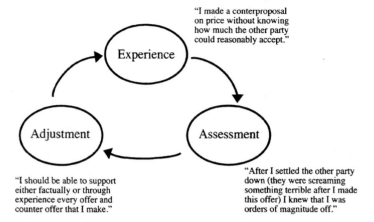

Figure 9.6

Learning Process in Negotiations

Let's learn from our mistakes and improve our responses and performance in negotiations. There is truth in the saying: "You can truly learn by failure and making mistakes." Let's ensure that we won't make the same mistake twice.

Use the six-step method for value-added results. Try it out in your next negotiating situation. Hone your skills in using the methodology. We assure you that with practice, you will become known as an excellent negotiator who achieves results which are acceptable to both parties.

Negotiating Style Questionnaire

A.1 NEGOTIATION QUESTIONNAIRE

Please complete the following questions, providing the requested level of detail.

1. What types of products and services do you either buy or sell?

   Products: _____

   _____

   _____

   Services: _____

   _____

   _____

2. How often do you negotiate the terms and conditions of sale?

   ❑ Always ❑ Most of the time ❑ Some of the time ❑ Seldom

3. What types of issues do you regularly negotiate?

   _____

   _____

   _____

   _____

   _____

4. In general, how prepared is the other party for negotiations?

   ❑ Very prepared ❑ Somewhat prepared ❑ Not prepared

5. What activities do you undertake to become prepared for negotiations?

   Please list: _____

   _____

   _____

   _____

6. Please rate the following negotiating styles in terms of frequency used by your counterparts.

   ❏ Hard-Aggressive   ❏ Soft-Cooperating

   ❏ Compromising   ❏ Win/Win

7. What styles are the most effective? (Please rank in order of effectiveness.)

   ❏ Hard   ❏ Soft

   ❏ Compromising   ❏ Win/Win

8. How do you ensure that you interests are made known to the other party?

   _____

   _____

   _____

   _____

9. How does the other party inform you of their interests?

   _____

   _____

   _____

   _____

10. How long does the negotiation process normally take?

❑ Less than one month   ❑ More than one month

❑ Less than two months   ❑ More than two months

❑ Less than three months   ❑ More than three months

11. Generally, how would you rate the results of your negotiations?

❑ Outstanding   ❑ Very Good   ❑ Good
❑ Fair   ❑ Poor

12. To what do you owe your negotiating success?

_____

_____

_____

_____

13. Could you describe in detail a negotiation "case study" which could indicate a glowing success?

_____

_____

_____

_____

_____

_____

_____

_____

_____

_____

_____

_____

13a. What were the reasons for this success?

_____

_____

_____

_____

14 . How about a negotiation "failure"?

_____

_____

_____

_____

_____

_____

_____

_____

14a. What were the reasons for this failure?

_____

_____

_____

_____

Thank you for your time and effort.

May we contact you?   ❏ Yes   ❏ No

Name: _____

Company: _____

Address: _____

Phone: _____

Case Studies and
Training Program Exercises

The information in this appendix is representative material used in typical Harris Consulting negotiation training programs.

Should you wish to use this material, simply complete the questions at the end of each exercise, evaluate, and discuss the results in a group setting.

Rate Your Performance Level: Negotiations and Conflict Resolution

	Needs Improvement (1–3)	Average (4–6)	Very Good to Outstanding (7–9)
Negotiations	• Does not consider other parties' interests. • Doesn't attempt to learn interests of conflicting parties. • Demonstrates only aggressive or uncooperative behavior. • Accepts or recommends acceptance of "win/lose" solutions. • Shows excessive emotion. • Rarely develops negotiation plan.	• Often demonstrates success in negotiations, but also evidences problems in achieving negotiated results. • Usually remains calm in negotiations, but at times, becomes emotional and even loses "cool." • Usually can understand what others need, but at times, exhibits "blind spots." • Advocates or accepts compromised results. • Can brainstorm solutions, but has difficulty in moving parties toward a common resolution. • Demonstrates cooperation, lacks aggressiveness to get parties to common ground. • Sometimes develops a negotiation plan.	• Remains calm and professional in negotiations. • Takes the initiative to identify key principles or needs governing a situation and finds ways to give everyone at least some of what they need. • Focuses on principles, not personalities. • Achieves successful number of results. • Advocates collaborative approach. • Works to achieve mutually acceptable solutions. • Develops action plans to achieve satisfactory results. • Can help parties control emotions. • Always develops a negotiation plan.

Circle those bullets which best describes your performance. Based on that tally, what is your overall assessment?

    1-3   4-6   7-9   (Circle One)

B.1 LIFE IN THE FAST LANE

Dan Tucker was facing his fourth straight week of intense planning and negotiation of parts to be included in the next version of Product X, a new product scheduled for full scale production in late 1994. His commodity, hybrid semiconductors, had been a hot topic due to the high expense and the limited supplier base for his key parts.

Tucker supported the South Attleboro manufacturing plant and was currently a senior buyer, just finishing his second year with the company. On his drive into the office on a balmy summer Tuesday morning, Tucker compared his current assignment with his previous buying position with a very large computer manufacturer in the Illinois area. The responsibilities of the job are essentially the same, he thought, but clearly the pace was quicker and more exciting than the previous one. We had an enormous pool of people to draw resources from, he lamented, but the process was so bogged down in approvals and bureaucracy, it took months to get a corporate purchasing agreement in place. At XYZ, the approval levels are reasonable and a person has more responsibility to get the job done and feels empowered to do so.

As Tucker was pulling into the parking lot, he suddenly remembered that an important meeting had been scheduled for this morning involving price targets for his assigned parts. "Now that's why I'm thinking about my old job," Tucker thought. "I've got a say in what is included in our product costs. The trick is to ensure that we negotiate the best deals with our suppliers and leave them with a good feeling about the results."

The Start of the Day

As soon as Tucker reached his office, he learned that the meeting was set for 11:00 AM. Great, he'd have about three hours to prepare! He pulled out the latest specification for the logic board for the Product X and found his most expensive part. "Let's see what the supplier has pulled together for me," he thought as he dialed the telephone number.

"Hello, this is Tim Roth," said the person at the other end. "Can I help you?"

"Tim, this is Dan Tucker from XYZ," Tucker responded. "I'm calling about that hybrid part we discussed last week . . . I think it was your Part Number 35657-BOHY."

"Oh, Hi Dan." Roth answered. "We have been working up the numbers for that part. It doesn't look like we'll be able to reduce the price too much from our quote."

"That's disappointing, Tim. We're counting on a major reduction so that the price we offer on the final product will be appealing to our customers," Tucker explained, as he noted the target pricing of $25.00/part. "You know how the thinking goes, Tim. The better price you can offer, the lower the price our customer pays. We sell more units as a result, which means we buy more units from you. We both sell more!"

"I've heard that story before, from your hybrid buyer in Scotland," Roth said, as his voice became louder and louder. "We cut our margins dramatically so that the average was 47% and the ROI was about 11.5%. Those cuts were based on receiving a certain quantity of orders for the part. Those orders never materialized, and we've lost a bunch of money. Consequently, we are going to structure a different type of deal for this new part, perhaps based on stairstep pricing or guarantees."

As Tucker listened, he wondered about the previous negotiations and how they might affect this one. He also was confused with the margin discussion and ROI. He hadn't studied those concepts since his financial management courses in college. Nonetheless, he still had to respond appropriately to the response from Roth. He wanted to be tough and aggressive.

"I don't care about the other agreements you've reached with XYZ. That was then. This is now. Let's start anew and keep focused on the lowest price for the ultimate customer, okay?"

"I thought you folks would communicate better. Aren't they a part of your purchasing department? Don't you discuss previous negotiation history?" Roth commented. "Look, we're absolutely not going to enter into another high risk situation with a new part without some protection on the downside. And that's final!"

"It's obvious we need to sit down on this one, Tim," Tucker indicated. "Can you at least give me some cost information so that I can discuss it with management?"

"It's not our normal practice but I'm willing to provide it to speed negotiations along, Dan," Roth replied. "Here's the breakdown:

Labor	$ 11.27
Overhead	6.37
Materials	4.58
Profit	9.00

"That makes the final tally about $33.00. Keep in mind that the price is contingent on receiving orders for 20,000 parts, split about 25% per quarter. Any questions?"

"Yeah, like what in the heck is overhead, and what makes up the materials number, and is the profit reasonable for this type of part," Tucker thought; "I'd better do my research before I respond to him."

"I've written down what you told me, Tim. I don't think management is going to like it," Tucker said, hoping for a revised proposal.

"These are the numbers, Dan. If you folks think you can reduce the price by improving our production processes, we'll entertain it." Roth responded. "Maybe you should ask someone else to give you a quote. I'm sure we'll be much lower."

"This is the favored supplier already," Tucker thought. "Plus the vice president of manufacturing loves them. We've just got to work something out."

"Okay, let me discuss your proposal with them and get back to you after our meeting," Tucker replied. "I'll call you back."

"Okay, but don't hope for miracles!" Roth said, as he hung up the phone.

With that, and after computing the effect on the manufacturing costs, Tucker went to the target pricing meeting.

The Meeting

As Tucker entered the conference room he noticed that the vice president was not present. Most of the other buyers and manufacturing representatives were there however. The meeting was going to be run by the director of materials.

"This will be an abbreviated meeting, everyone," Tom Davis said as he opened the meeting. "I don't have to remind you that Product X is an important product for XYZ. We will sell this product almost as a commodity, so our offering price has to be absolutely the lowest possible."

"That means we have to push our suppliers hard on price," Dick Levine, purchasing manager indicated, interrupting Davis. "Purchasing will do its part to give the lowest price."

"Thank you, Dick," Davis responded. "As I was saying, the C . . ."

"Now wait a minute, Tom," Mary Tolbert, quality manager interjected. "I just have to respond to Dick's point. I thought we were going to focus on negotiating the best overall value to XYZ when negotiating with our suppliers. Ultimate purchase cost is only part of the equation . . . the other pieces include financial terms, delivery and quality history, warranty, reliability, responsiveness, and ease of doing business."

"I know best value is something we discussed, but do we really need to implement it on Product X?" Levine answered.

"Of course, we should start it on a high volume product because the return is there," Tolbert remarked.

As the discussion went back and forth, Tucker began to consider how the concept of best value would apply to his critical part. How would he compute it, and what was the impact of computing it on a single source part? As he was considering it, the discussion in the meeting switched to decentralized manufacturing and interplant cooperation.

"As I was saying, we need to be sure that whatever pricing arrangements are struck, they are appropriate for the entire company," Bill Bragg, commodity manager said. "Let's ensure that we work with all the plants to roll up their requirements for the different markets. Let's also bundle parts together with the same supplier and negotiate a corporate-wide purchasing agreement with the goodies that Mary was espousing."

"This is a new concept for us, and how it is applied is important given the decentralized nature of our business today," Davis indicated. "Can you give us an example of how this is going to work?"

"I'd be glad to, Tom," Bragg responded. "Take the hybrid semi on the logic board. That represents about 12% of the cost of materials."

What! Tucker's mouth dropped. "That's my part. I can't believe it."

Bragg continued. "I've been negotiating with the president of that division. We've had two meetings. I've thrown in all the other hybrids and the microprocessors we buy from them. We've established quality and reliability goals and they are considering holding some parts in a buffer inventory for us. They want a 55% margin on the account as a whole and we're talking with them about their manufacturing costs for the new hybrid and introducing some process improvements. The talks are really at a high level and we are making progress."

"How long have you been working with them?" Tucker inquired, hoping for a logical answer.

"Since my visit to the coast last month, Dan," Bragg responded. "We purposely didn't want to get you involved until we reached an initial understanding of our goals."

"That's interesting, Bill," Davis commented. "But it seems that you did not include everyone in the loop. You need to get Dan and others involved in the process at this point. Now for our last topic. Let's see if the suppliers would be willing to locate an assembly point near our production plants for Just-In-Time deliveries. They also might be willing to share some of the development costs if we allow them to sell some of our design ideas to other companies that are not direct competitors. Well, that's all I have. The only final action item is to ask for your plans for negotiating key parts by the end of the week so that the VP and I can review and comment on your plans. Any questions?"

By this point, Tucker was even more confused. He had so many questions on this but where should he start? Who should he involve? How should he now work with Scotland and Bragg? What should the negotiation plan look like? How should he ensure that the entire company's needs are satisfied? He just left the meeting shaking his head and hoping for a quick remedy.

B.2 QUESTIONS

1. What negotiating issues are brought up by this case? Do these issues exist at your company? Which ones and why?

2. How did Tucker and Bragg get themselves in this position? What could they have done differently in the planning phase?

3. How can Tucker ensure that the company's interests are satisfied?

4. How would you approach the negotiation at this point? Who would be involved?

5. How would you respond to Roth's proposal? What other information might you need?

6. What are the elements of the negotiation plan that Tucker and Bragg need to develop as they plan to continue negotiations with the supplier?

7. How would the six-step model be applied in this situation?

B.3 BUYER SIDE NEGOTIATING FOR THE PLASTIC MOLDING–XYZ CORP.

Dave Johnson, Senior Vice President for Precision Molding Inc. (PMI) called XYZ to confirm the upcoming negotiations meeting in early February with a friendly gesture, saying to the XYZ buyer, "Thank you for agreeing to meet with us. Maybe after we complete negotiations, we can all take a cab to the North End for some Italian food."

Agnes Devine, the XYZ buyer, had immediately responded, "Dave, thanks for your offer but the way that this negotiation has gone so far, I don't think either one of us will want to eat after we negotiate."

Johnson was surprised with the response from XYZ, given the quality of the relationship and the degree of support given to XYZ up to that point.

Background

PMI is a company with annual sales of approximately $160 million. They specialize in designing, developing, and manufacturing a wide variety of plastic molding enclosures for applications in the defense/aerospace and automotive industries. XYZ uses PMI products in a number of its divisions worldwide, and for the past five years has entered into corporate-wide agreements with the company.

PMI is considered to be a leader in its field. It was also one of the early suppliers to XYZ as the company was growing. So naturally, XYZ was pleased to have PMI as a manufacturer of some if its key parts. One of the key parts was the X34 enclosure which was to be integrated into XYZ's end product to be supplied to Honda.

The X34 drawing was first supplied to PMI in early 1989, and a price of $24.00 per assembly was negotiated. The forecast of volume was to grow significantly over the ensuing years based on Honda usage of the final product as follows:

- 1989-250,000
- 1990-500,000
- 1991-750,000
- 1992-600,000
- 1993-500,000

Prices were negotiated annually, based on the automotive model year which runs from July to June. After initial negotiations in 1989, the price for the part had been increased from $24.00 for the 1989 model year to $26.00 for 1990 to $28.00 for 1991.

The negotiations process typically started in the fall of the year preceding the introduction of the new models. So, negotiations for the 1992 model year would start in the fall of 1991. Negotiations for the X34 would be managed by the Framingham plant, leaving the balance of parts to be included in the corporate-wide agreement to be negotiated by corporate purchasing. These negotiations normally occurred in the spring of each year.

Historical Perspective of Negotiations to Date

Devine had led the negotiations with XYZ since the inception of the project. The negotiations had always been tough, even bitter, in the past because PMI had always been reluctant to fully support their positions. PMI had mostly used a strong, aggressive approach and sometimes resorted to a take-it-or-leave-it approach to negotiation proposals and counter-proposals.

Some PMI personnel (particularly engineering) on the negotiations team, felt that PMI representatives were making up stories. The general feeling about Johnson was that he did not share information readily and exhibited suspicious behavior.

Devine was suspicious about PMI's motives from day one. This was due to the fact that every time he spoke with Johnson, Johnson complained about the pricing for the X34 and made comments such as "These prices are killing me," or "I'm losing money every time we negotiate for these parts." XYZ had always tried to pass on the limitations in its Honda contract, which were based on guidelines of 3%-2%-2% annual decrease for the first three years of the contract.

The X34 was part of the end product which XYZ sold to Honda for $240, so the cost of the MCU had to be kept to an absolute minimum. Since PMI was the leader in the field and presumably had the best technology and cost position, they should have been able to provide the lowest price for the part.

In the summer and fall of 1991, PMI began to miss shipments of its orders. These delinquencies were mostly confined to four to seven calendar days. Devine calculated that it cost XYZ about $500 per missed delivery due to expediting costs and delays. The quality of the X34s being shipped was also declining. Defects were associated with packaging problems and blemishes, both caused by procedures being performed too hurriedly.

In late 1991, Devine was shocked to receive a letter from PMI requesting a meeting in two weeks to discuss a price increase as well as other items. The letter contained three specific items as follows:

- Convert other new plasmold material and process within two months. (This would be impossible because XYZ would need to qualify the new process and receive Honda's approval, which could take up to six months. A significant amount of data would be required from PMI.)
- PMI wanted to outsource the X34 whenever they were required to do so to meet the schedule. (Some of the potential sources were in Mexico. Honda wanted to source most of their sub-contracted parts in the U.S. so this could become a thorny issue from that standpoint as well as require XYZ to qualify the new source directly.)
- Last, and more importantly, PMI requested a 45% price increase, from $28.00 to $40.00 per piece part. (The request was not justified and was presented in typical PMI fashion—take it or leave it. The request was unconscionable because it would drive the XYZ cost of material through the roof and reduce its already low margin.)

Devine knew that she would have to prepare data to counteract and even contradict the PMI request. So she set off investigating sources throughout the U.S., requesting bona fide bids to provide the part using the agreed upon volumes. Devine and the engineering manager traveled extensively, explained the part to the potential suppliers, and requested the kind of backup information necessary to substantiate the prices received.

The following information was tabulated:

Average prices (includes direct costs and profit margin)

Molds	6.70/part
Components	7.25/part
Assembly	8.00/part
Other Costs	1.80/part
Total	$23.75/part

Devine was pleased with this information and intended to use it effectively in the upcoming negotiations. Devine and her team reluctantly felt that up to a 5% increase would be acceptable but knew that XYZ could not pass on any price increase to Honda. They would have to justify the increase to the general manager in any event.

In speaking with the rest of the negotiating team, it was determined that XYZ would work with PMI if they indeed wanted to outsource but would insist on qualification and a cutover schedule as well as advance notice requirements. They would also be willing to negotiate the use of plasmold technology, but would need to alter the schedule to comply with Honda's requirements. Both of these issues would be used as trade bait to counteract the price increase request.

XYZ was contemplating building the X34 module itself to ensure control of supply and cost, as well as fill the in-house manufacturing capacity and costs. This could result in lower annual volumes. The X34 had the high volume that XYZ manufacturing preferred, but Devine knew that that might jeopardize pricing and delivery of other products being sourced with PMI.

XYZ was also requiring suppliers of sheet metal to consider locating a manufacturing or at least an assembly plant near its other plants in the U.S., Mexico, and Europe. Devine wasn't sure of PMI's likely response to this issue. Devine also felt that XYZ had an option to source the X34 with the other quoted sources but needed to retain PMI for at least the balance of the model year and whatever time would be required for Honda to approve the new source. Devine now must plan for the upcoming negotiation in the first week of February.

B.4 QUESTIONS

1. What are the driving forces in this negotiation?

2. What are the potential points of disagreements?

3. How might XYZ have contributed to this problem?

4. What are XYZ's objectives in the upcoming negotiations?

5. What are the components of your plan?

B.5 SELLER SIDE NEGOTIATING FOR THE PLASTIC MOLDING–PMI

Dave Johnson, senior vice president for Precision Molding Inc. (PMI) called XYZ to confirm the upcoming negotiations meeting in early February with a friendly gesture, saying to the XYZ buyer, "Thank you for agreeing to meet with us. Maybe after we complete negotiations, we can all take a cab to the North End for some Italian food."

Agnes Devine, the XYZ buyer, had immediately replied, "Dave, thanks for your offer but the way that this negotiation has gone so far, I don't think either one of us will want to eat after we negotiate."

Johnson was surprised with the response from XYZ, given the quality of the relationship and the degree of support given to XYZ up to that point.

Background

PMI is a company with annual sales of approximately $160 million. They specialize in designing, developing, and manufacturing a wide variety of plastic molding enclosures for applications in the defense/aerospace and automotive industries. XYZ uses PMI products in a number of its divisions worldwide, and for the past five years has entered into corporate-wide agreements with the company.

PMI is considered to be a leader in its field. It was also one of the early suppliers to XYZ as the company was growing. So naturally, XYZ was pleased to have PMI as a manufacturer of some if its key parts. One of the key parts was the X34 enclosure which was to be integrated into XYZ's end product to be supplied to Honda.

The X34 drawing was first supplied to PMI in early 1989, and a price of $24.00 per assembly was negotiated. The forecast of volume was to grow significantly over the ensuing years based on Honda usage of the final product as follows:

- 1989-250,000
- 1990-500,000
- 1991-750,000
- 1992-600,000
- 1993-500,000

Prices were negotiated annually, based on the automotive model year which runs from July to June. After initial negotiations in 1989, the price for the part had been increased from $24.00 for the 1989 model year to $26.00 for 1990 to $28.00 for 1991.

The negotiations process typically started in the fall of the year preceding the introduction of the new models. So, negotiations for the 1992 model year would start in the fall of 1991. Negotiations for the X34 would be managed by the Westboro plant, leaving the balance of parts to be included in the corporate-wide agreement to be negotiated by corporate purchasing. These negotiations normally occurred in the spring of each year.

Historical Perspective of Negotiations to Date

Johnson had led the negotiations with XYZ since the inception of the project. The negotiations had always been very intense from a pricing point of view. XYZ had always indicated that Honda was imposing heavy cost targets for its end item, so the cost of the X34 had to be kept to a bare minimum. The guideline of 3%–2%–2% annual decreases for the first three years was mentioned in the negotiations as a requirement that XYZ had to live with in the prime contract with Honda.

PMI had originally provided a low price to XYZ so that they could eventually apply their newest technology to the production of the part. This technology was not planned to be on-line until late 1990 or early 1991, and even if the new technology was not on-line at that point, PMI felt that they could subcontract or outsource the product to companies that could produce the part perhaps more economically using the older technology. The margin on the product was low:

- 1989 Direct Cost   .50
  Margin   .32
- 1990 Direct Cost   .53
  Margin   .31
- 1991 Direct Cost   .55
  Margin   .31

When agreeing to these lower prices, Johnson recognized the creeping increases in direct costs and the lower profit margin percentages but was hoping for the plasmold breakthrough to reduce the direct costs and provide a higher margin on the plasmold parts.

In late 1991, plasmold capability was finally online. At this point in time, Johnson was taking some pressure from management to improve margins, and in fact, from time to time had made decisions to delay the production of XYZ X34 parts in favor of higher margin products. He knew that XYZ was somewhat disappointed at PMI's shipping delinquencies. He also knew that quality problems had crept up due to the concession of some of their production lines to the plasmold technology.

He commissioned the PMI purchasing department to determine the real market value for the part being supplied to XYZ. He believed that they were in a leadership position since they had provided the part to XYZ over the last three years, and XYZ and Honda would be reluctant to change suppliers at the same time that production requirements were doubling.

The results of the purchasing study were very illuminating; as the quotations received from three U.S. qualified suppliers averaged about $34.00 per part and from two companies in Mexico they averaged $18.75 per part. Purchasing had asked its suppliers for a budgetary quote based on the older technology. He couldn't believe the great deal that XYZ was receiving. He began to devise a strategy to increase the price to XYZ based on this new information and the availability of the new technology which could lower the price by 10% or more.

In fact, Johnson had talked to Devine in late 1991 about the delivery problems and had mentioned to her at that time that prices would have to increase because he simply was not making any money.

The Strategy

In preparation for the meeting to occur in early 1993, Johnson devised the following plan:

- Request that XYZ approve transitioning to the new plasmold material and process within two months. (He expected some resistance to this time frame because of the lengthy qualification process imposed by XYZ and Honda, but he knew that for every month delay, it could cost PMI $2.00 per part.)
- Outsource the product to plants outside the U.S. to relieve PMI of growing costs and capacity problems in the older process. (At present, PMI could only produce about 2,000,000 parts per month on the entire line using the older technology, but had other customers who required output from that line and who had higher quoted prices.)
- Propose a 45% increase to $40.00 which would take advantage of their strong sole source position and leverage the more expensive quotes received from purchasing.

Johnson sent XYZ a letter outlining these issues and hoped to conclude negotiations on the subject in their upcoming meeting, in two weeks.

In his telephone conversation with Devine, she told him that they were asking more and more suppliers to set up local manufacturing or assembly operations near XYZ plants. Performing a quick analysis of this option, Johnson calculated that the tool alone would cost $50,000 and the minimum fixed cost to set up an assembly operation would be about $1,500,000 plus variable costs of manufacture.

B.6 QUESTIONS

1. What will XYZ's likely response be to the price increase?

2. How might PMI have contributed to the problem?

3. What will XYZ's objectives be?

4. What long-term benefits will you be seeking?

5. What are the elements of your plan?

B.7 ANALYZING NEGOTIATION SITUATIONS

An important part of the negotiation planning process is to determine which approach is most suitable given the facts in the situation at hand. This is traditionally the case when buyers and sellers are attempting to negotiate. Does the advantage rest with the buyer or the seller? The answer to this question frequently determines the style that the buyer must use in approaching the seller, in order to arrive at a fair and reasonable agreement on price, delivery, or any other issue.

The following pages briefly describe nine situations. Your task is to review the facts in each case and to come to a conclusion as to where the negotiation advantage lies in terms of power, information, and time. After you have reached a position on each situation, indicate your answer in the space provided. Be prepared to explain the rationale for your choice and whether the advantage is due to power, information, and/or time.

1. The facilities department has requested the purchase of ten copying machines designed for self- service in various locations. The machines must be capable of single-feed, single-sided copying and automatic sorting. A brief review of trade literature reveals a number of brands of machines that meet this broad specification.
   Who has the advantage?

	Power	Information	Time
Buyer			
Seller			

2. You have been buying shipping cartons printed per your instructions and made to your specs for three years from Andrew's Packaging Company. Andrew's has produced over one million cartons per year for you and has maintained the same price each year. Your requirements contract is about to expire. You are going to issue a call for competitive quotes, but one of the prospective

bidders has told you informally that the industry is aware of your contract with Andrew's and that no one is optimistic about bidding against Andrew's this year.

Who has the advantage?

	Power	**Information**	**Time**
Buyer			
Seller			

3. You are trying to fill an order for about $50,000 worth of spare parts for several computers. You prefer not to go to the original manufacturer because the price has been prohibitively high in the past. You are aware that these parts are available from several distributors. In the past, these distributors have been able to underbid the manufacturer on some of these parts.

Who has the advantage?

	Power	**Information**	**Time**
Buyer			
Seller			

4. The media department has sent you a purchase request for the services of two software engineers for a four month assignment to design a new accounts payable system. The job requirements are well detailed, as are the qualifications for the needed personnel. You know of three firms in the area that are capable of supplying qualified people on a contract basis.

Who has the advantage?

	Power	**Information**	**Time**
Buyer			
Seller			

5. A member of the marketing department requires the use of photo-
graphic services for some product literature development. The
requisitioner has specified that photographer Milt Jones be used
because Jones employs a particular lighting style that is unique. He
has also been closely identified with your product illustrations in
the recent past.

Who has the advantage?

	Power	Information	Time
Buyer			
Seller			

6. You have received a request for the purchase of catering services
for an important function for your company. A buffet dinner and
beverage service for 500 people is required to be held ten days
from now. You are aware of at least three firms whose services you
have used successfully in the past. Unfortunately, they all require
two weeks of lead time to handle a major event such as this.

Who has the advantage?

	Power	Information	Time
Buyer			
Seller			

7. You have received bids for 20 pieces of calibration equipment from
the three most qualified firms in the industry. However, two of the
firms have stated that they cannot meet your delivery schedule
because of other production commitments and that they would
require a slippage of two months from your stated schedule. A
check with the requisitioner reveals that while it is not impossible, he
would prefer not to change the established delivery schedule.

Who has the advantage?

	Power	**Information**	**Time**
Buyer			
Seller			

8. You are placing an order for fax machine suppliers to support the sales force. The suppliers are commercial brand-name products available from distributors. Lately, most of these products have been purchased from Tristate Enterprises, which seems to have a price advantage over other distributors. However, you have learned that several other suppliers would be able to offer competitive prices if your purchase quantities were larger or if you made longer term commitments. You are tempted to try to break Tristate's position since the company has started to become somewhat careless in meeting delivery schedules.

Who has the advantage?

	Power	**Information**	**Time**
Buyer			
Seller			

Bibliography

Albrecht, Karl and Steve Albrecht. 1993. *Added Value Negotiating.* Business One Irwin, Homewood, IL.

Barlow, C. Wayne and Glenn P. Eisen. 1983. *Purchasing Negotiations.* CBI, New York.

Calero, Henry H. and Bob Oskam. 1983. *Negotiate the Deal You Want.* Dodd, Mead, New York.

Cohen, Herb. 1980. *You Can Negotiate Anything.* Lyle Stuart, Inc., Secaucus, N.J.

Edelman, Joel and Mary Beth Crain. 1993. *The TAO of Negotiation.* Harper Business, New York.

Fisher, Roger and William Ury. 1981. *Getting To Yes.* Houghton Mifflin Co., Boston, MA.

Griffin, Trenholme, J. and W. Russell Daggat. 1990. *The Global Negotiator.* Harper Business, New York.

Hanon, Mack, James Cribbin, and Howard Berrian. 1977. *Sales Negotiation Strategies.* Amacom, New York.

Harris, Charles Edison. 1983. *Business Negotiating Power.* Van Nostrand Reinhold Co., New York.

Ilich, John. 1973. *The Art and Skill of Successful Negotiation.* Prentice Hall, Inc., Englewood Cliffs, N.J.

Ilich, John. 1980. *Power Negotiating.* Addison-Wesley, New York.

Karrass, Chester. 1970. *The Negotiating Game.* Thomas Y. Cromwell Co., New York.

Kennedy, Gavin. 1983. *Everything is Negotiable.* Prentice-Hall, Inc., Englewood Cliffs, N.J.

Kennedy, Gavin. 1994. *Field Guide to Negotiation.* Harvard Business School Press, Boston, MA.

Kennedy, Gavin, John Benson, and John McMillian. 1980. *Managing Negotiations.* Prentice-Hall, Inc., Englewood Cliffs, NJ.

Kennedy, Gavin, John Benson and John McMillan. 1982. *Managing Negotiations.* Prentice-Hall, Inc., Englewood Cliffs, NJ.

Kennedy, Robert F. 1969. *Thirteen Days.* Wms. Norton, New York.

Lax, David A. and James K. Sebenius. 1986. *The Manager as Negotiator: Bargaining for Cooperation and Competitive Gain.* Free Press, New York.

Levin, Edward. 1980. *Negotiating Tactics: Bargain Your Way to Success.* Fawcett Columbine, New York.

Levitz, Lon. 1987. *No-Fault Negotiating.* Warner, New York.

Lewicki, Roy, J. and Joseph A. Litterer. 1985. *Negotiation.* Irwin, Boston, MA.

Maccoby, Michael. 1977. *The Gamesman.* Bantam Books, New York.

Morison, S.E. 1949. *History of U.S. Naval Operations in World War II.* vol. IV, Little, Brown, Boston, MA.

Nierenberg, Gerald, I. 1968. *The Art of Negotiating.* Cornerstone Library, New York.

Nierenberg, Gerald, I. 1973. *Fundamentals of Negotiating.* Hawthorn Books, Inc., New York.

Raiffa, Howard. 1982. *The Art & Science of Negotiating.* The Belknap Press, MA.

Schatzi, Michael and Wayne R. Coffey. 1981. *Negotiations.* The New American Library, Inc., New York.

Seltz, David D. and Alfred J. Medica, 1980. *Negotiate Your Way to Success.* Farnsworth, New York.

Sheppard, Pamela and Benedicte Lapeyre. 1993. *Negotiate in French & English.* Nicholas Brealey, London.

Sperber, Philip. 1983. *Fail-Safe Business Negotiating.* Prentice-Hall, Inc., Englewood Cliffs, N.J.

Stark, Peter B. 1994. *It's Negotiable.* Pfeiffer & Co., San Diego, CA.

Warshaw, Tessa Alberg. 1980. *Winning by Negotiations.* McGraw Hill, New York.

Zartman, I. William and Maureen R. Berman. 1983. *The Practical Negotiator.* Yale University Press, New Haven, CT.

Index